Learning to Enjoy Literature

Learning to Enjoy Literature

How Teachers Can Model and Motivate

Thomas M. McCann and John V. Knapp

ROWMAN & LITTLEFIELD
Lanham • Boulder • New York • London

Published by Rowman & Littlefield
An imprint of The Rowman & Littlefield Publishing Group, Inc.
4501 Forbes Boulevard, Suite 200, Lanham, Maryland 20706
www.rowman.com

6 Tinworth Street, London SE11 5AL, United Kingdom

Copyright © 2021 by Thomas M. McCann and John V. Knapp

George Grosz's drawing "Fit for Active Service" is reprinted by permission of the Museum of Modern Art, New York, New York.

Gary Soto, "Like Mexicans" from *The Effects of Knut Hamsun on a Fresno Boy: Recollections and Short Essays*. Copyright © 1983, 2000, by Gary Soto. Reprinted with the permission of Persea Books, Inc. (New York), www.perseabooks.com. All rights reserved.

Chris Ware's drawing "Stop," March 14, 2016, *The New Yorker*, reprinted by permission of Chris Ware.

All rights reserved. No part of this book may be reproduced in any form or by any electronic or mechanical means, including information storage and retrieval systems, without written permission from the publisher, except by a reviewer who may quote passages in a review.

British Library Cataloguing in Publication Information Available

Library of Congress Cataloging-in-Publication Data

Names: McCann, Thomas M., author. | Knapp, John V., 1940- author.
Title: Learning to enjoy literature : how teachers can model and motivate / Thomas M. McCann and John V. Knapp.
Description: Lanham : Rowman & Littlefield, [2021] | Includes bibliographical references and index. | Summary: "This book offers teachers productive approaches to treating textual interpretation not as an effort to reach a single right view or answer, but rather as a collaborative activity involving lively discussion of texts drawn from a variety of media"— Provided by publisher.
Identifiers: LCCN 2021007267 (print) | LCCN 2021007268 (ebook) | ISBN 9781475860214 (Cloth) | ISBN 9781475860221 (Paperback) | ISBN 9781475860238 (ePub)
Subjects: LCSH: Teaching—United States. | Teachers—Training of—United States. | English teachers—Training of—United States. | Literature—Study and teaching (Secondary)—United States.
Classification: LCC LB1025.3 .M34565 2021 (print) | LCC LB1025.3 (ebook) | DDC 371.102—dc23
LC record available at https://lccn.loc.gov/2021007267
LC ebook record available at https://lccn.loc.gov/2021007268

To our many students, who have patiently alerted us about the classroom experiences that foster understanding and pleasure from reading literature.

Contents

Preface: Learning to Enjoy Literature—How Teachers Can Model and Motivate   ix

Acknowledgments   xiii

Introduction   1

1   Don't Go There   5

2   Why Do We Have to Read This?   17

3   Preparing for the Literature Experience   25

4   Noticing and Making Meaning   47

5   Modeling, Sharing, and Practicing   61

6   Seeing Patterns and Structures and Making Complex Inferences   79

7   Considering Competing Critical Views   95

8   Responding to Literature   109

9   Expanding Conceptions of Literary Texts   125

Appendix: Gary Soto's "Like Mexicans"   141

References   145

Index   149

About the Authors   155

Preface

Learning to Enjoy Literature—How Teachers Can Model and Motivate

Thomas M. McCann and John V. Knapp, coauthors of this volume, have known each other for a half century and have enjoyed nearly 100 years, collectively, of English teaching experience at many levels, from middle school to doctoral seminars at the university. Some years ago, Tom had proposed to coauthor with George Hillocks, one the luminaries at the University of Chicago in English education scholarship, a book on foundational needs and problem in teaching secondary English. Unfortunately, before they had completed much more than a proposal, George passed away after a long illness, leaving a grief-stricken Tom with little more than fond memories of his mentor and a proposal.

He determined to continue the work as a *homage* to George Hillocks and invited his NIU English Department colleague, John, to join in completing the task. The result was their book *Teaching on Solid Ground: Knowledge Foundations for the Teacher of English* (2019), a book whose chapters focus attention on many aspects of teaching English language arts. It was indeed meant to be, with all due modesty, a foundational book on teaching English.

They were pleased with the result and hoped that George would have been pleased as well, looking down from heaven and noticing many of his teaching ideas inside their completed labors. Consequently, Tom and John both thought that they would like to go further into writing about teaching English. More specifically, they were interested in continuing to develop some newer and more expansive ideas into the teaching of literature. These would be teaching strategies employed in ways that reflected research not often seen in other books and articles aimed for aspiring secondary English teachers and/ or for those in their early instructional careers.

In particular, Tom noted how much research in the teaching of writing had developed by leaps and bounds over work done in the previous decades before the turn into the twenty-first century. He wondered why that research seemed in many ways more sophisticated than that of secondary literary research during the same years of the new century. John, as longtime editor of the literary journal *Style*, also speculated why there was such a large gap between literary analysis published in *Style* and in those essays appearing in journals aimed at secondary literature teachers. This gap was not always explained or answerable by asserting secondary students' differing developmental levels and maturity, although younger students comprised the audience that secondary teachers encountered in their everyday classrooms.

Hence, for a number of reasons, Tom and John decided to write a second book, *Learning to Enjoy Literature: How Teachers Can Model and Motivate*, but this one would emphasize primarily the teaching of literature, one that included storytelling not only in print formats but also with stories relayed in graphic novels with pictures and/or illustrations. It would include tales in verse, like Homer's *The Odyssey*, as well as prose narratives, and in films so that "literature" in this book could well stand for stories conveyed in a variety of media. Given the popularity of the Internet and games played on electronic computers of all types, John and Tom believe it is of crucial importance that students continue learning the knowledge bases and skills associated with literacy generally and with imaginative literature specifically. In the Internet age, they must develop and so join in the cultural vocabulary of educated members of the voting citizenry.

For thousands of years, those who have lived longer speak to the youth of all ages via stories and tales of the past and present. Those who are mature know full well that wisdom and knowledge are found in stories, poems, and problem-solving experiences in the past and in the imagined future are often as useful and as appropriate in the present as they were "back then." While students must of necessity occupy the present, most realize, after reading good literature, that lessons about wisdom and knowledge may be readily learned once they have acquired the skills needed to decode and understand the great literary texts that may initially have seemed dated and irrelevant. Indeed, in literature, we have written and filmed evidence that human beings have wrestled with problems of living, loving, and learning not totally different from and no less important to them than those our students face today.

Among the most important lessons secondary students experience and so learn in well-taught literature classes include those of developing empathy for characters, an emotional growth of particular importance when students encounter characters they do not like nor understand very well. These feelings for characters are then explored by the whole class as the teacher wisely engineers discussions and then stands back to listen and guide as readers share emotionally based storytelling insights. Such activities often help growing teens learn to treat one another with greater respect and sympathy.

In addition, debates on interpersonal and group conflicts in stories and films help sharpen students' critical thinking skills, analyze stubborn conflicts, discuss value differences, and, in some stories, look at characters both from the past and the imagined future. Teachers hope that novice readers learn to cope with and interact sensitively with those they meet in various narratives, even if the worlds in which characters had to live were very different from their own.

Another lesson, as important as any, is the combination of students' building vocabulary and becoming more fluent in argumentation and verbal expression. Some students come from environments where English may not be spoken, and/or where some homes cannot afford newspapers, books, magazines, and other popular teachers of reading literacy. While TV and the Internet provide some alternatives to students' reading, electronic media used for their educational values may not be, nor perhaps should not, one could argue, be the primary learning source for in-depth analysis and lengthy examinations of complex issues.

As it now stands, electronic media can provide students entertainment from stress-filled workdays and, as well, survey-like explanations on many political and/or philosophical issues. However, media rarely can encourage students to participate in depth-filled examinations of life in the ways that social experiences in a book-centered classroom debate can provide. For thousands of years, those qualities have been among the reasons why most child-rearing adults have spent so much energy, time, and fortune on equipping their offspring with the tools needed in learning how to read and enjoying the life containing literature and storytelling in all its various forms.

The present book, in acknowledging all of the above, is aimed particularly at teachers-in-training, at teachers currently on the job in the schools, and at any adult wishing to learn how and why their children are being instructed as they are now or even should be by those who have read Tom and John's books. They bring to this conversation years not only of their own continued education but of new learning as they publish peer-reviewed work both of theoretical and practical research in teaching literature and storytelling. Their work also includes also many years of helping and training those soon-to-be-licensed secondary English teachers. Much of their own personal excitement comes from observing trainees' growth and development—from nervous and unsure novices into maturing and competent leaders of a classroom containing restless adolescents. Tom and John are hopeful that this book helps their teachers with some necessary skill-building activities to that end.

Acknowledgments

We owe a debt of gratitude to Peter Rabinowitz and James Phelan for helping us to think not only about how narratives work but how we might take a somewhat novel approach to helping adolescent readers to read complex works of literature in a way that mature readers approach such texts. We are also grateful to Michael W. Smith and Jeffrey D. Wilhelm for their work in helping adolescents to think beyond the conventional conceptions of literary elements and for suggesting us an instructional sequence that would help students to become aware of procedures for reading literary texts and transfer those procedures to increasing complex works.

We are grateful to Chris Ware and Gary Soto for their generosity in allowing us to reprint their work for the purpose of helping teachers of literature to advance their craft. We thank the staff at the New York Museum of Modern Art for consenting to the reprint of George Grosz's drawing "Fit for Active Service." We also appreciate the generosity of Ezzat Goushegir in allowing us to recount an episode from her memoir. We thank Genevieve Sherman for helping us to access resources that we needed to complete the book.

The examples of instructional activities in this book come from lessons we have taught and we have shared with colleagues. We appreciate the insightful critical comments from Elizabeth Kahn, Carolyn Walter, Beth McFarland-Wilson, Shannon McMullen, and Gabrielle Caputo. We have also gained much from the insights of master teachers Joseph Flanagan, Dawn Forde, and Andy Bouque.

John V. Knapp thanks his generous and talented coauthor, Thomas M. [Tom] McCann, for inviting him once again to join a project creating pedagogical books that we trust will be helpful to teachers of imaginative literature in the secondary schools across North America. We both are grateful to many of our colleagues, former students, and friends who have stimulated our writings, employing the somewhat modified ideas of other scholars of literature teaching, notably those of the late George Hillocks, and to many contributors to the journal *Style*, too many to name here. We have all profited from their engagement with what Matthew Arnold once referred to as "the best that has been thought and said."

Furthermore, we want to acknowledge the support of family and the many lessons they have taught us. John thanks his daughters Margaret A. Knapp; Lara M. Cantuti and husband, Eric; Joanna E. Haskin; and Jennifer Joy Schmeiser and husband, Brian, and is grateful to his grandchildren for showing such happy energy to their grandparents: Steph'ane John-Georgio Cantuti; Jack Amadeo Salzberg; and Abi Joy and Emily Joy Schmeiser. John also thanks his loving wife, Joan I. Schwarz, his companion and educational partner over many years of stimulating conversations.

Tom McCann appreciates the genial and reliable collaboration with his long-term mentor and colleague John Knapp. Tom acknowledges with gratitude the support of his dear wife Pam, his daughter Katherine Carlson, and her husband Alex Carlson, all of whom have contributed insights into how to influence students to become enthusiastic readers of literature.

We also thank editor Dr. Tom Koerner from Rowman & Littlefield Publishers. We are grateful for his appreciation of the merits of the project and for his attentive work in advancing the book from initial conception to finished product. We also appreciate the contributions of the many hands of the editorial and production staff at Rowman & Littlefield, especially Carlie Wall and Meaghan Menzel, for their careful attention to the refinement of this work.

Introduction

In his 1993 National Council of Teachers of English (NCTE) research report on the teaching of literature in secondary schools, Arthur Applebee lists the common practices of the day. Popular at the time was teachers assigning students a text to read at home and then attempting a discussion on the next day. This routine was commonly accompanied by quizzes. The discussions themselves were a means for assessment. Students also wrote as a means of assessment: full essays with the "college prep" students and short written responses with the "non-academic" classes. Teachers reported other instructional activities: writing in journals, completing worksheets and study guides, and occasionally dramatizing a scene from the literature (Applebee, 1993, pp. 116–38).

In the Applebee study, teachers reported that they judged it was important for all students to engage in discussions. The teachers reported that it was important for the students in the "non-academic" classes to complete worksheets and to read aloud. Teachers embraced the idea that it is important for students to read independently. Teachers occasionally used films to support the study of literature.

These dominant practices—assigning reading, quizzing students, prompting recitation or discussion, and completing worksheets—remain in place today. Of course, teachers and students more recently have relied on technology and media, especially digitized versions of texts, discussion boards, and online communication. In the end, however, the experience in most classrooms, middle school through college, is that the teacher assigns students to read a text that the teacher or a curriculum committee has deemed important as part of students' cultural experience and assess students through quizzes and recitation as a means for motivation to read or as a check on comprehension. With the adoption of the Common Core State Standards in many states, there has been a return to a New Criticism spirit with an the emphasis on "close reading," often attempted in a vacuum that disregards the life of the author or the historical context in which the author produced the text. Missing in this dominant routine is attention to *teaching students how to read*, especially by demonstrating the discipline of reading complex literary texts and by immersing students in purposeful practice in the procedures for reading such texts.

Certainly, demonstrating a few intellectual moves involved in reading and then structuring opportunities for students to practice these moves will not be sufficient and are not likely to inspire an enthusiasm for reading literature. At the same time, worksheets, turn reading aloud, quizzes, and recitations are likely to inspire a distaste for reading complex works of literature. But, at the core, where teachers need to change for the sake of their students is to reveal the *procedures* that highly literate people practice as they engage with a text. As a beginning, many students need to see how the reading of a complex text is an active effort at constructing meaning. Lining up a series of questions in a study guide, introducing literary terms, and packing students' homework with vocabulary words to look up will not lead students down a path of inevitable understanding of what they have read, nor will requiring students to visualize, predict, and question while they annotate texts in detail. These common practices do not reveal how skilled readers construct meaning from a text and appraise the author's implications. In fact, these popular practices reveal the study of literature to be burdensome and boring.

This book offers some alternatives to the pedagogical practices that still dominate in schools and universities. Certainly, teachers work very hard and in good faith to influence students to read literary texts and appreciate them. The dominant practices that teachers have observed for years must influence their efforts to deliver instruction in a bona fide way; that is, in a way that everyone else seems to be doing. The alternative practices recommended in this book draw from cognitive science and from scholarship in narratology. From a cognitive science perspective, a teacher needs to consider how a reader reads any text. From a rhetorical perspective, a teacher needs to appreciate how literary texts, especially narratives, are typically constructed, recognizing that the features that someone sees on the page or the screen of an electronic device are the product of some author's conscious effort.

This book asks readers to consider the various approaches that teachers take to teach literature and to assess the assumptions behind those approaches. The chapters of this book suggest ways that teachers can prepare learners for their reading, especially when texts will seem quite complex to the learners and when a teacher judges that students will benefit from either tapping into prior knowledge or building the necessary background knowledge. At the core of the recommended practices is attention to "rules" associated with how narratives are constructed and how highly literate readers work with the texts—*rules of notice*, *rules of signification*, *rules of configuration*, and *rules of coherence* or *unity* (Rabinowitz, 1987; Rabinowitz and Smith, 1998). Lectures about these concepts are practically useless, but students do benefit from seeing how a mature reader *notices* features of a text, assigns meaning or interrogates the implications of these features, and recognizes how texts are configured and when the common configurations are ruptured.

As the book models, it is helpful to meet students where they are—often in popular media—and proceed systematically from relatively simple texts to increasingly complex texts. We presume that in most instances, teachers licensed to teach English will be more experienced and knowledgeable than their students when it comes to reading literature. As Graff (1992) points out, students often see their literature teachers as people who are especially adept at "finding hidden meaning" from texts. This aspect of reading literature seems a mystery to many learners. This book suggests that it is time for teachers to expose what they know about reading literature so that students can recognize some reliable procedures and reflect on their own processes for constructing meaning from texts.

Part of the pleasure of experiencing literature is the sharing with peers. This book encourages a move away from recitation and a move toward genuine discussion. This is an important distinction to make, with recitation serving as a form of assessment of recall and discussion serving as an exploration of ideas. As the chapters of this book demonstrate, there are identifiable pedagogical moves that will foster discussion, and the rich discussion in the classroom or online can position students to offer elaborated and meaningful written responses to the texts that they study.

A key element of preparing students for their reading and for facilitating conversations about texts involves helping students to be aware of multiple possibilities, as viewed through several lenses for interpreting the reading. In fact, the chapters of this book will demonstrate that without an awareness of differences in judgments and appraisals about texts, it is near impossible for students to write meaningful analyses about what they have read. The book features activities that help students to become familiar and comfortable with considering competing views of texts so that they can frame interpretive problems when they write and become accustomed to reacting to conflicting views with reason and civility.

Taken together, the many recommended practices in this book are intended to reveal what mature readers do, engage learners in meaningful and rewarding discourse about their reading, and encourage a rationale response to alternative views: all this in the cause of fostering an enthusiasm for reading literature and encouraging a lifetime of experiencing and sharing literature.

Chapter 1

Don't Go There

On Tuesday morning, Ms. Merrick directed her ninth-grade English class to access Guy de Maupassant's short story "The Necklace" on their tablets. On the white board at the front of the room, Ms. Merrick drew a diagram, with a line moving from left to right and then rising upward and to the right, and then a shorter line declining from the peak to the right and then leveling off. Ms. Merrick paused to direct the ninth graders to take notes, first by copying the diagram. She then labeled the diagram with descriptors: exposition, rising action, climax, falling action, and denouement. Ms. Merrick then directed her students to recall the action of "The Necklace" and note the specific events and responses in the story that corresponded to the descriptors on her diagram. Some students grumbled; some looked confused; one said out loud, "Why do we have to do this?"

This scene repeats itself in one form or another in thousands of classrooms across states, despite new possibilities suggested by theory and research and regardless of contemporary practices sponsored by the National Council of Teachers of English and other professional educator organizations. If reflective teachers put themselves in the place of some weary ninth graders in Ms. Merrick's classroom, they might share several questions: Why do we have to read fiction, especially stories selected by the teacher or by some anthology editor? What good is studying literature at all? Why can't we just read the story for the experience of it, rather than having to label parts and recall answers about it? Do all short stories follow the pattern that the teacher has imposed on this one?

These are some tough questions, and Ms. Merrick as well as other English teachers will have to construct answers for themselves and want to find ways to help learners discover the value in the study of literature. If students are to enter into meaningful dialogue about texts, they will need to embrace the idea that the effort to construct meaning and to make critical assessments is worthwhile. Not every classroom discussion will be richly engaging, but if more often than not, conversations about reading and storytelling become stimulating students will inspire each other's reading. To help achieve some literary play, the teacher must exhibit flexibility as an important attribute in classroom teaching: that is, the ability to react to the interesting questions that often arise spontaneously from students who may be frustrated or bored or confused with the methods of analysis the teacher uses and procedures that may have solidified the teacher's approaches to a given text or genre over some years.

If we view ourselves as teachers of literature and hope to engage learners in the study of literature, presumably we have a keen sense of what this endeavor is. From a university perspective, Scholes (1998) asks teachers what they hope to accomplish by teaching literature. Is the idea to help learners to tell the story of the development of literature? Anthologies like the popular Norton series would suggest this is the case, with texts arranged in chronological order so that a consumer of the selections can see that one text or author followed another and perhaps the predecessor exercised some influence. Many who have studied the selection process understand that the choices made are not always selected on purely artistic merit, and one critic argues that the editors may have had more mundane, even mercenary reasons why they picked one author or selection as opposed to another (Shesgreen, 2009).

An experienced teacher of literature may well begin a class with an easily read short story (e.g., Soto's "Like Mexicans"), a reminiscence of a now well-respected and famous author, but try to move the learners along as they grow in their ability to consider such issues as narrative voice, unusual voice tones, and visual focalizing in stories. Your own version of Ms. (or Mr.) Merrick will continue to challenge you, helping you to look at a more extensive vocabulary, more sophisticated sentences and paragraphs, and greater complex human interactions, exchanges that you will add to and internalize with your own life stories to help with understanding.

Perhaps the study of literature involves the attentive consumption of not-to-be-missed masterpieces so that readers have these cultural icons under their belts as marks of educational distinction. This seems to be a dominant sympathy in middle school and high school. Text choices could include the attentive consumption of "not-to-be-missed masterpieces": *Hamlet*, *Pride and Prejudice*, *Great Expectations*, *Huckleberry Finn*, *Moby Dick*, *The Bluest Eye*, and so on. There is much value in all humanistic fields, and the study of literature is as foundational as any in the humanities. The study of literature remains of crucial importance for adolescents who may have doubts about the value of expending considerable time and energy on complex texts—for whatever payoff the reader is supposed to experience.

Reading stories and debating their values "often invites readers' empathy," as Susanne Keen believes. In an appendix to her *Empathy and the Novel* (2007), she lists some twenty-seven hypotheses that invite thinking that reading helps develop the reader into a more empathetic soul. Some appear to contradict each other, and here are two examples:

1) Character identification often invites empathy, even when the character and reader differ from each other in all sorts of practical and obvious ways. (167)
2) *Bounded strategic empathy* operates with an in-group, stemming from experiences of mutuality, and leading to feeling with familiar others. (170)

So, we may be "hooked" by someone(s) like us, or very different from us. Keen suggests that "the contract of fictionality offers a no-strings-attached opportunity for emotional transactions of great intensity. A novel-reader may enjoy empathy freely without paying society back in altruism" (168).

Another view would offer that *the study of literature involves the learning of disciplined procedures for constructing meaning from complex texts and evaluating them as works of art and as arguments about politics, esthetics, philosophy, and human behavior*. Although our text choices may be different, serious thinkers operate on mastering a piece of writing, a work of art, an oral-based story, or a serious film in roughly the same way as others in the humanities do—philosophers, historians, art and film critics—as they exercise their levels of expertise. The idea in this view, and one often missing in schools, is that for students to commit themselves to the study of literature, two conditions must be present: (1) students have to recognize some value in exerting any effort in constructing meaning from complex texts, and (2) teachers have to teach explicitly *how* to read complex literary texts and not simply assign reading. This book offers some possibilities for teaching students *procedures* for reading complex texts and reflecting on, and responding to, those texts critically.

WHAT IT ISN'T

A reader might begin by saying what the study of literature isn't. Before you complete your reading of this chapter, you are likely to consider what the study of literature is and examine an overview of the principles that teachers can follow to make the study of literature coherent, appealing, and meaningful. First, the name of the teacher Ms. Merrick and others in this book are pseudonyms. The teachers profiled in the book are composites of several teachers, including the authors. If some depictions poke a bit of fun at teachers, they also poke fun at the authors who have often stumbled over the years through many attempts to make the study of literature appealing and meaningful for our students.

As a beginning point, it seems obvious that what Ms. Merrick is doing in our opening scenario is not the study of literature. She may be doing what she saw English teachers do when she was in high school or what some of her more experienced colleagues have endorsed. In other words, she may be imitating what she has seen others do (cf. Lortie, 1977). She may also be following the recommendations from a teacher's manual that accompanies a textbook. In this case, Ms. Merrick's efforts are misguided. While readers in any specific culture will have conceptions of ideal story structures and use that knowledge to organize recall, Freytag's pyramid is definitely not a reliable representation of stories in general. In fact, Freytag's pyramid is one critic's representation of nineteenth-century European drama.

Perhaps, Ms. Merrick's goal is to help students in naming parts of a story, especially as a device to help in recalling the plot. But if the point is to assign reading and expect learners to recall details of the story and the pattern of the action of the narrative, there are other ways to support recall. The reaction of the students in Ms. Merrick's classroom reveals that her approach—assigning a story, naming the parts, requesting notes-taking, and testing for recall—is neither an engaging way of studying literature nor a viable way to teach literature.

What attracts most students of fiction reading, on the one hand, are the characters and the personalities in the tale as familiar or strange as they appear at first (Vermeule, 2010). Getting familiar with these characters, the reader begins feeling empathy, and some sympathy or even anger at something they've done. As a reader, you become invested in the problems they (and the author) have to try to solve to keep your attention and help make your experience so interesting that you are reluctant to put the book down.

As your familiarity with similar problems in a given genre—say the hardboiled detective novel—increases after reading many different Marlow-type investigations, you consider now the author and the tale itself; you begin to match wits with the author trying to predict who really did kill the reclusive millionaire. What you are quite likely to NOT get excited about is labeling and naming "literary techniques," or listing all the metaphors of animals in chapter 3, and "stuff" like that. You don't have to have extensive experience with adolescents to know that they find this kind of school-ish activity insufferably boring.

Let's imagine the logical extension to Ms. Merrick's instruction. For the next class meeting, Ms. Merrick assigns students to read Richard Connell's "The Most Dangerous Game." As students anticipate the bell at the end of class meeting, Ms. Merrick's warns obliquely that "You never know but there might be a quiz on the story." In a sense, Ms. Merrick's quiz serves as a threat and is supposed to motivate students to actually read the story. To some extent, fear often is a motivator in the classroom. But such fear lasts only so long, and is not the key to forming positive relationships with learners.

Once out of school, students may never take another quiz again, nor, sad to say, read another novel or poem just for pleasure. If the quiz asks students to recall details about the narrative (e.g., Who is the *protagonist*? Who is the *antagonist*?), then the assessment rewards memory above all, even when the teacher never taught students *how* to recall. The instructional approach acknowledges that students will be reluctant to read and they need the teacher's threats to influence them to read. This hardly seems the formula for building enthusiasm for the reading of literature. The approach also neglects the *teaching* of the reading of literature and relies instead on the *assigning* and the *assessing*, especially with using the assessment as a threat.

Of course, Ms. Merrick is one of many teachers. Consider her colleague Mr. March in the same department. He has assigned students to read Langston Hughes's "Thank You, Ma'am." In class, before the students began their reading, Mr. March explained some details about the Great Depression, showing some vintage photographs on PowerPoint slides, and playing some recorded jazz music typical of music pervading Harlem in the early 1930s. When Mr. March assigned the reading, he provided students with a set of "guide questions" to direct their reading and to prepare for a discussion.

The next day, Mr. March invited the students to access the story and he initiated a discussion. Here is a bit of the exchange:

Mr. March: Where does the story likely take place?
Vince: It's like a city somewhere.
Mr. March: It's probably New York, and specifically Harlem. When does the story take place?
Amber: Do you mean like what year, or what time of day?
Mr. March: Either one.
Amber: I don't know what year, but a long time ago. It's at night, cause the lady is coming home from work and hasn't had supper yet.
Mr. March: As we talked about yesterday, it is probably taking place in the early 1930s, still during the Great Depression. And you're right, it is evening, when Mrs. Jones is on her way home from work, which makes the attempted theft all the more annoying to her. What reason does Roger give for trying to steal Ms. Jones' purse?
Vince: He said he didn't mean to, but he obviously meant to steal it. Then he says he wants some blue suede shoes. Is he serious?

Mr. March: That style of shoe must have been popular among some young people at the time, and Roger wanted to be in style. So, I would say that he was serious about that. So, what happens when he tries to steal the woman's purse?
Amber: He falls down and she kicks him and then gets him into a headlock.
Vince: A half-nelson, when you put your arm around someone else's arm and then put your hand on the back of the person's neck. Want me to show you?
Mr. March: No, thanks, Vince. When Roger is in Mrs. Jones' room, he has an opportunity to run away. Why doesn't he?
Vince: He's scared. She already had him in a half-nelson once and she kicked him in the rear. He probably thinks she could catch him and rough him up.
Florence: I don't think so. She could have turned him over to the police, but she doesn't. I think the kid figures that she means him no harm, so he'll stick around because he feels bad about what he did.
Mr. March: So, Roger probably recognizes that Mrs. Jones is trying to help him in some way. He is a bit afraid of her, but he recognizes her good intentions. At the moment, especially if this is during The Depression, Roger probably isn't getting much sustenance and comfort at home, and Mrs. Jones is probably the closest thing to parenting that he has experienced.
Florence: Well, I don't think we know that. He might be very poor and he sees things advertised that attract him, but his parents might be doing the best they can.

Mr. March engages students in discussion about the story. The discussion would suggest that the multiple readers have had a variety of experiences with the text, and through the sharing of those experiences, they all appear to have come to a deeper understanding of the text. At least, the dialogue puts readers in a position to examine their impressions and assumptions about the story. But Mr. March's discussion is a bit uneven. It begins with recitation, with the teacher asking for the answers he already knows (what Nystrand [1997] calls *pre-specified answers*): the setting of the story, the given reason for the attempted theft, and the viability of the stated reason.

Then the students examine a more open and complex question about a character's motivation for acting, or not acting in this case: Why doesn't Roger run away? To answer the question, students have to be familiar with the events in the narrative, understand something about human behavior, interpret the actions and character of Mrs. Jones, and read the behavior of Roger. The question invites multiple possibilities, and the interchanges among readers would likely help them to have a rich picture of Mrs. Jones's attitude and intentions, and Roger's response viewed through historical, cultural, and psychological lenses.

For all of the promise in Mr. March asking an interpretive question, he limits the possibilities by endorsing a particular view and elaborating on that view. Despite his obvious skills in initiating the discussion, Mr. March reduces the dialogue to recitation. In a sense, Florence does him a favor by challenging his assumptions about Roger's family. If Mr. March were to embrace this contradiction, the discussion could help everyone to refine their understanding of the complex of factors that influence both Roger and Mrs. Jones.

As emphasized in detail in a later chapter, discussion can enrich students' experience with a text and can help them to become aware of the procedures at work when a mature reader reflects on a work of literature. As Timothy Shanahan (2013a, 2019) reminds us, the dangers we would want to avoid are the "guide questions" that limit and narrow readers' experiences with the text, and the reliance on the same two or three eager students to contribute the bulk of the responses. These twin flaws in a particular classroom conversation often lead to the descent from discussion to recitation, with the teacher rather than the students offering most of the analysis.

Down the hall from Ms. Merrick and Mr. March is Mr. Reingold. In his classroom, he has assembled a modest library, supplied mostly with young adult novels, but including biographies and some magazines. Mr. Reingold doesn't *teach* literature, per se, but he allows students to read freely and independently. Acting on the belief that students will cultivate an enthusiasm for reading and will naturally develop skills at reading by reading the texts that interest them, he schedules at least one class meeting each week to devote to sustained silent reading. Sometimes he allows students two class meetings in a week to read whatever they want.

Occasionally, Mr. Reingold selects a text that some of his students have responded to enthusiastically and asks the whole class to read it. This common reading allows for a whole class discussion, usually prompted by the students' questions and by the responses from some of the more outspoken members of the class. When asked about holding students accountable for having read a substantial amount, Mr. Reingold responds that he asks students to write about their reactions to a text in their reading journals, which he reads from time to time without actually grading. Mr. Reingold reports that he sees that students are reading and he talks to them about their reading, so he is little concerned about "accountability" and grades in a conventional sense.

Mr. Reingold is patient and idealistic, yet an observer might question his use of so much valuable instructional time for sustained silent reading, especially if most of his students are reading a steady diet of a single subgenre of young adult literature. Much of what they read in Mr. Reingold's class, they can very well read on their own, as so many Emiles educating themselves by following the whims of their hearts and pursuing their enthusiasms. If there is a discipline to reading mature literature and Mr. Reingold has some expertise in this area, then he is obliged to demonstrate what mature readers do by engineering specific environments that allow his students to practice the procedures that he demonstrates, especially with the kind of dialogue that Mr. March attempts to foster in his classroom.

Another member of this diverse faculty is Ms. Bindings. Since she is teaching the AP Literature and Composition class and hopes to prepare students well enough for them to earn scores that can bring them college credit, she requires the reading of the kind of texts that are valued on the AP exam: for example, texts by Shakespeare, Jane Austen, Toni Morrison, William Faulkner, Cormac McCarthy, and several notable poets.

Ms. Bindings focuses on the test. In a recent lesson, she introduced her students to the eight types of questions commonly found on the multiple-choice portion of the AP exam, and students practiced with some sample items. Keeping in mind the possible "open" questions that students might see on the exam, Ms. Bindings chose titles that would support discussion of a variety of essay questions—from explorations of familial relationships to conflicts about revenge and justice. The students have occasional discussions about their assigned readings, and Ms. Bindings checks for the accuracy, substance, and logic of their responses. Her students also practice a series of timed essays, responding to questions that mimic the type found on the AP exam.

There is no doubt that Ms. Bindings knows a good deal of literature and probably has some expertise in reading literature carefully and critically.

Table 1.1: Instructional Emphases and Their Assumptions

Teacher	Emphasis	Assumptions
Ms. Merrick	Assign and assess	The important thing is to force students to read what they are assigned to read and to *recall* what the teacher judges are the essential elements of a narrative: characters, setting, and plot.
Mr. March	Pathfinding	The teacher has already read the text and has a solid understanding, so his job is to preview the reading and ask sets of questions to *guide* learners down the path that he has already cleared.
Mr. Reingold	Discovery	Given an opportunity to follow their own inclinations and enthusiasms, whatever they might be, students will ultimately learn something about literary texts and learn more generally just from the *experience* of reading.
Ms. Bindings	Preparation for assessment	Since students are taking a literature class to prepare them for an exam for which they might earn college credit, the appropriate place to apply their energy is to recognize the demands of the exam, build a stock of literature experiences, and practice the moves necessary for *performing well* on the exam.

However, Ms. Bindings has become a kind of technician, embracing the self-imposed obligation to prepare a select group of learners to perform well on a test designed by other technicians. These test creators may not be engaged in providing stimulating questions to facilitate student growth, but often are hired by a company whose business creates discriminators. Discriminating questions are composed to sort out students by means of a timed exam, with benchmarks that predict how well the students would likely do if they actually took a literature class in college. Ironically, the idea of scoring well on the test means those students can avoid taking any literature classes after high school.

Perhaps the teachers profiled here do not look anything like the teacher you are or the teachers you know, but they are common to schools across America. Some instructional models are to be avoided, because they don't help students to learn and they don't foster enthusiasm for reading literature. Table 1.1 summarizes four popular stances in regard to the teaching of literature. What are the alternatives?

AN ALTERNATIVE VIEW

An alternative approach could be called a *cognitive-rhetorical* model for teaching literature. The table of contents of this book serves as an outline for the model. It is *cognitive* in the sense that drawing on a foundation from cognitive science and reading research allows teachers to take advantage of the processes that serve readers in their attempts to follow along with a narrative, recall it as a cohesive whole, and connect the text to other narratives and to life experiences. The approach is also *rhetorical* in the sense that a reader can assume that the author of a story or a drama works *intentionally*, and an attentive reader can notice the elements that the author likely expected the readers to notice and then construct meaning about these features of the text, based on the rules for assigning meaning to patterns, images, symbols, and even punctuation.

The focus in this book is on the teaching of narratives—stories, novels, and elements in plays—even though there is much more to literature than these broad categories. The reality, however, is that most of the literature studied in high school is fiction and drama. The study of poetry is important as part of one's literary experience as a whole, but it requires its own book and someone else's expertise. Recognizing the reality of conventional literature curricula in schools, this book focuses on the study of narratives. Here, then, is an overview of the sequence on which the following chapters expand.

A SEQUENCE FOR LITERATURE STUDY IN HIGH SCHOOL

Prepare readers for their encounters with a text by activating prior knowledge or building background knowledge. The pre-reading activities serve many purposes: prompting some interest in the reading, helping readers to process the text by connecting a presumably new text to information stored in memory, fostering empathic responses to the characters, cultivating the critical language for engaging in dialogue about the text, and introducing interpretive questions that might drive the reading and prepare learners for discussions and written responses.

Model procedures for noticing key features of a text and conjecturing about their implications, and then *facilitate practice* with the procedures.

Engage readers in discussions to explore the implications of a narrative or drama, keeping questions authentic and allowing students to grapple and stumble a bit as they attempt to construct meaning.

Introduce competing critical views of a work to expose students to extended possibilities seeing implications and for judging the qualities of a text.

Experience a narrative or drama in performance to consider the nuances in specific scenes and appreciate a scene's connection to a broader pattern across a work.

While the following graphic representation of the process of teaching literature is a simplification of a complex endeavor, it offers a convenient overview of how a teacher can approach the teaching of literature with adolescents, and there are references to this summary throughout the book.

Figure 1.1 represents the study of literature as a simple, linear process. The components of the process sometimes overlap, reorganize, and are often recursive. Both reading and discussion can activate prior knowledge, and a reader might naturally view the work through several critical lenses. This figure is a rough road map, and the teacher who relies on it, asking students to write about their readings and/or using it as a guide for them, should be responsive to current conditions, and to one's own students' skills and abilities.

Any reader, including both teacher and students, might be thinking about possible written responses to the text as he or she is making a way through the reading, so an end goal often influences the reading experience. An even more writing-intensive thinker, Gary Weismann (2016), maintains that

> it is one thing to interpret a text while reading it, and then while musing over what one has read, and quite another to interpret it in writing [. . .] a time-consuming, isolating, and stressful activity, particularly when we know others will be reading and judging what we write.

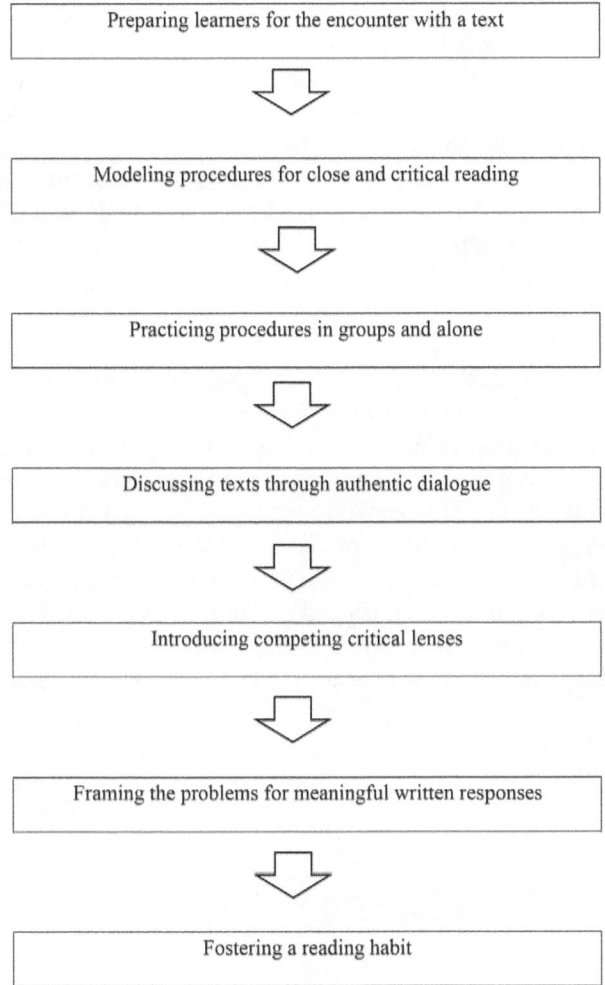

Figure 1.1 A Sequence for Teaching Literature.

Weismann argues that "literary interpretation is practiced less in the act of reading a text . . . than in the act of rewriting it by telling a story about its significance or meaning" (26).

Individual teachers will have to decide how much reading and writing about reading their students will do as part of their total literacy experience. The expectations for assessment and performance by the end of work with a particular text will influence teachers in how they prepare students for their reading and discussions.

In addition to this pattern of instructional practices, in later chapters, the book treats how to work with alternatives to conventional print texts as literature, suggests ways to encourage a reading habit and an enthusiasm for reading literature, and illustrates ways to prepare students for meaningful written responses to texts. The next chapter moves into the instructional processes and invites teachers to think about the question a student posed in Ms. Merrick's class: "Why do we have to do this?" If a teacher is going to engage groups of adolescents in reading complex texts and studying literature, the teacher better have a firm idea of what she is trying to do with learners and why the endeavor is important.

Your View

Perhaps you see something of value among the four teachers profiled earlier, or perhaps you disagree with the assessment of them. You might also recognize that the profiles of just four teachers neglect to showcase another approach to the teaching of literature that you judge to be far more engaging to learners and beneficial to their learning. It will be a constructive experience for you to write your own theory or vision of literature instruction. As a rule, it will be hard to engage learners when you don't have a solid conception for what you are trying to accomplish and a plan for how to accomplish it. You need to discover what will stand up to the scrutiny of other reasonable persons by sharing your vision with peers and discussing your intended approach and theirs.

Chapter 2

Why Do We Have to Read This?

Anyone who has had any experience in teaching literature in high school has encountered at least one bold and candid learner who asks, "Why do we have to read this stuff?" In this context, "stuff" often refers to a Shakespeare play or to poetry or to other texts that present their own challenges because of vocabulary, syntax, or presumed cultural or historical understandings. Various commentators and literary figures have spoken eloquently about the value in the study of literature. But each teacher has to answer this core question for himself or herself, and needs to answer the question in ways that might persuade adolescent learners.

If teachers cannot share cogently with others the value they see in reading and studying literature, then the teaching of literature becomes a hollow endeavor and assigning students to read particularly challenging texts becomes an almost sadistic action. Typical responses fall under three categories: esthetic, pragmatic, and intellectual. Of course, these three elements intersect, since an esthetic response requires the intellect; our critical encounters with literature can have pragmatic ends.

LITERATURE AS ENTERTAINMENT

Lifelong readers of literature of all kinds enjoy becoming immersed in the reading of a good book or the viewing of a compelling play. In the same way that adolescents might sit in a theater watching the next installment of a superhero series or binge-watch online dramas, readers of literature surrender themselves to enlightenment, horror, humor, irony, novelty, romance, reversals, shocks, surprises, sentiments, and more. These experiences give us pleasure and leave us wanting for more.

Some of the pleasure is visceral, and it is difficult to put into words the delight in the experience, just as someone might be swept away emotionally by a brilliant piece of music or a masterfully executed painting. But the delight is also intellectual as the reader sees value in creativity, the sophisticated use of language, and the power of nuanced thought. Of course, one person's pleasure might be another's torture; just ask any couple who attempt to negotiate a film to watch at the theater or a program to view on television.

It is difficult, then, to persuade learners to appreciate the esthetic experience of reading a text that they find difficult or unappealing. Reading carefully, critically, and reflectively involves procedures developed over time, going far beyond simple letter and word decoding, and requiring use of one's critical faculties to make sense of many interactive combinations. The reader must continue to acquire a broad vocabulary, sentence-level syntactical sophistication, and the lifelong development of understanding of meaning and tonal qualities on the printed page or its digital equivalent. In our own time, types of media employed in storytelling have broadened beyond the wildest dreams of teachers and literati from barely a century ago.

Our task as literature teachers is to equip our students with the skills they'll need to navigate among print tales, graphic novels, and multimedia texts mixing pictorial or visual representations and print generally. Like it or not, our tasks ahead are, in part, bridging exercises and demonstrating the value and the joy of reading texts while, at the same time, acknowledging the virtues of storytelling on screens or through audio devices. We can begin by creating synergistic activities, lessons combining the best of both types of pleasurable intellectual and emotional experiences.

LITERATURE STUDY AS THE BUILDING OF READING SKILLS

We might appeal to our learners that the careful reading of texts is in their own self-interest. If readers have not developed skills at reading contracts closely and critically, they are likely to fall victim to deceptive practices. If readers or listeners do not see logical fallacies and other rhetorical efforts to manipulate thinking, they can fall victim to demagogues and unscrupulous marketers. Perhaps students are singing along with songs that run counter to their beliefs or are eager to buy the aggressively advertised products that do them harms while promising to make them more appealing and successful. Some students might see a kind of survivalist value in reading carefully, but they have a hard time seeing how the close reading of *Macbeth* or selections from *Paradise Lost* will prepare them to scrutinize a car rental contract or the ads of hair care and skin care products.

LITERATURE AS EMPATHIC EXPERIENCE

It is easy to imagine readers taking pleasure or satisfaction in reading a narrative about a character with whom they share some similarities or from a place familiar to them or involved in a circumstance that they recognize. There is a kind of reassurance and implied sympathy when someone reads about characters who have shared the same problems they have faced or harbor the same feelings that they have about themselves and others (Vermeule, 2010). There is a kind of power in following the story about characters who have shared the same situations, doubts, and conflicts, and a reader might find satisfaction in seeing that someone can work through some difficulties that have vexed them.

There is also a value in exploring new worlds through the dramas a reader/viewer experiences and the narratives they read. While no one should ever expect to experience life in a concentration camp or the aftermath of the explosion of a nuclear weapon or a voyage upon a whaling vessel in the pursuit of deadly behemoth or a perilous journey to save a village from destruction, readers extend themselves by entering voluntarily into these imagined worlds. In a more modest way, readers also extend themselves when, through their reading of literature, they experience what it is like to grow up with an immigrant family in an impoverished area of a big city, to work on the killing floors of a meatpacking plant, to socialize among the wealthy elite of the eastern seaboard, or to endure the challenges of living on the Nebraska plain in the nineteenth century.

The wide, diverse reading of literature allows us to meet a variety of humans and experience a variety of cultures, communities, and situations. And, as we speculate about "nonjudgmentally entering the private perceptual world of the other," as the psychotherapist Carl Rogers would put it (Rogers, 1975, pp. 2–10), we may jump to consider our own place in the world.

LITERATURE AS EXPLORATION AND LEARNING

Skeptics might find it curious that anyone would devote a career to teaching students how to read fiction and to pursue a program of scholarship focused on imagined narratives. A sympathetic figure might question, why any would devote time and thought to stories that are "not true?" One reason is that the study of literature teaches much about life as the reader sees and experiences how others have faced conflicts and prospered or suffered based on the responses to those conflicts. But it might seem pathetic that anyone would hope to learn about life from reading fictions.

The study of literature or even the casual reading of novels and plays teaches readers much about many things—history, human psychology, geography, animal behavior, music, economics, cooking, gardening, and auto repair, to name a few. Often the reading of a work of fiction prompts readers to read other texts, both fiction and nonfiction. Simply put, the reading of literature contributes much to our ongoing education, even if that education is not a strategically designed program of learning.

Often our reading involves us in thinking in a rich exploratory way about core questions about our existence. One of the attractions of reading or viewing a Shakespeare play is that the playwright introduces a compelling question—for example, what does it mean to be human?—and examines the possibilities from a variety of angles so that at the conclusion of a performance or our reading, not only do we have a deeper understanding about some answers but we are also left with some additional questions to discuss with others or to mull over on our own.

Even a casual reader could summarize the plot of *Moby Dick* in a few sentences, but the experience of reading the novel involves more than following the pattern of the action. The richness of the experience includes our thinking about life's balance between woe and delight; about our perceptions of reality, goodness, and evil; about our connection to nature and to other humans; and about our compulsions and aspirations. Part of the pleasure of reading, then, includes the intellectual "work" that has readers delving deeply into conflicts, problems, questions, and presumptions.

While adolescents in their high school English classes might wonder why they are required to read literature, especially literature written more than 100 years ago, seldom do teachers offer the learners any rationale. One quick answer has to do with ordinary human understanding. As we read to learn about ourselves, we also absorb information about "the other." In doing so, readers find a developmental reward for attention to storytelling. Psychologist Zahn-Wexler (1992) found in her study "repeat occurrences or exposure can build a sense of familiarity that can overcome the bias against feeling for those who are dissimilar" (28: 126–36). Such findings echo an older and much-cited study by Robert Zajonc (1968) titled "The attitudinal effects of mere exposure." In what is now a commonplace in the psychological literature, these studies suggest, to say it in a simplified way, that the more we learn about others—through literature and even mere exposure—the more empathetic we may become.

Most adolescents are compliant in school, following along with the assignments and prescriptions because that is the way school works: teachers assign and learners do what is assigned. Of course, there are many implied reasons for reading the assigned texts: because the assignments are part of an established curriculum, because students will be tested on their assigned reading, because the reading will prepare them in some way for college, or simply because the teacher told them to. Some of these reasons suggest rewards, and some represent threats. In behaviorist language, the compulsion to read literature is that one will be rewarded for doing so or punished for failing to read. That's a model for training our pets not to relieve themselves in our homes. If we care anything for the learners, we have to do better than this.

LITERATURE STUDY AS INQUIRY

Smith and Wilhelm's (2002) study reveals that many adolescents whom teachers presume are nonreaders or reluctant readers actually have rich literacy experiences, just not the ones sponsored by their teachers. For many adolescents, the important motivation for reading is that it offers some utility: for example, how to move to the next level in a video game, how to fix some issues, or how to program something. That pragmatism might extend to problem-solving with the experiences of everyday living: that is, learning how to respond to many of the conflicts, conundrums, and dilemmas that life throws at us. While Wright's *Native Son* will not teach us how to change the oil in our car, the novel can help us to interrogate our prejudices and advance the cause of justice within our own community.

Graff (1993) recalls his experience in high school, where he was mystified by teachers' facility at "finding hidden meaning," but an awareness of adults' disagreements about how to read and appreciate *The Adventures of Huckleberry Finn* aroused in him an interest to read the text to discover what the conflict was about and where he might position himself in the conflict. Perhaps Graff's experience is not universally shared, but it does reveal a common response from many adolescents. While students might be reluctant to read the assigned acts in *Macbeth* and *Romeo and Juliet*, they would eagerly join in conversations about why apparently normal people commit hideous crimes or what true romantic love is and whether or not adolescents are capable of experiencing it.

In these situations, the conversations about compelling questions or problems provide a gateway into some complex texts. In some ways, an inquiry approach turns conventional practices upside down: instead of starting with the complex text, a class starts with a complicated and compelling problem. In other words, our inquiry into problems that our high school students found consequential served as a context and reason for tackling some texts that adolescents often find difficult. As part of inquiry into aberrant human behavior, a class examines what a thinker like Shakespeare or Twain or Wright or Achebe had to say about the problem. In the process, the teacher and learners link together several texts in one continuous and connected inquiry and conversation.

Hillocks et al. (1971) long ago presented an alternative to the conventional and widespread way of teaching literature through a teacher's presentations, which were attempts to transmit to learners what a teacher knew about works of literature and their authors and what a teacher judged to be an accurate appraisal of a work's merits. The alternative was what they called an "inductive" method of teaching and what Hillocks would later refer to as an "inquiry" approach to instruction and learning. Here is how Hillocks, McCabe, and McCampbell saw *induction* or *inquiry* working:

> Picture such a classroom. Students are actively engaged in discussing subject-matter problems with the teacher and other students. Most students participate in the discussion. At times students work independently; at other times they work in groups. They examine additional materials and discuss them. Gradually, having learned to approach problems of a particular type, they no longer need the guidance of the teacher in that respect. (p. 101)

There are two distinctive elements in this description of an "Environment for Active Learning." One is that students are interacting frequently, both in small groups and as a whole class. The second is that students are learning the *procedures* for some aspect of literacy: for example, analyzing a text and arguing to explain an interpretation.

In her report on schools that are "Beating the Odds," Langer (2001) uses different language to echo the position of Hillocks, McCabe, and McCampbell. Langer notes that among the schools that consistently outperform other cohort schools, students participate frequently in "instructional conversations" and engage in "generative learning"—the kind of learning that learners can apply in subsequent situations: in other words, *procedural knowledge*.

For many teachers of literature, and consistent with Hillocks and Langer, studying literature should engage learners frequently in the interactions with peers and through independent effort that will allow them to practice the adaptable procedures that they can apply again with new texts and in new situations. In addition, Langer notes that students thrive with a coherent curriculum, one in which the various texts and components connect, and the teacher can make the connections explicit from day to day and week to week. This is consistent with Hillocks, McCabe, and McCampbell's earlier vision of teaching coherent literature-based units of instruction in which study of language and composition integrates naturally with the explorations with literature.

Table 2.1 below outlines the common rationales for the teaching of literature that we have represented in this chapter. We discuss an *inquiry* stance last

Table 2.1 Purposes for Studying Literature

Purpose	Value
Entertainment	The reader becomes involved in a "story world" that offers delight in thrills, surprises, humor, lyricism, tensions, exotic settings, and so on.
Skill Building	Practice with reading a variety of texts helps learners to advance their various literacy proficiencies.
Empathy	The reader can project him-/herself into the life of the characters and appreciate their problems, challenges, and accomplishments, leading to introspection, so that looking at others' inner selves often includes looking at one's own inner feelings and thoughts.
Content Learning	With experience with a variety of literary texts, the reader inevitably learns content—about history, politics, art, ethics, philosophy, and so on.
Inquiry	Readers engage with each other in thinking deeply about problems that they find compelling.

because this is the one we admit is our preferred approach. After decades of teaching, we feel that we have tried just about every instructional possibility and conclude that *inquiry* offers the promise of *coherence* and *engagement*. As you will see in chapters 4 and 5, we have selected examples of work with texts that students can connect to each other as part of a broad investigation into a compelling problem.

LITERATURE AS ALL OF THE ABOVE

We have reviewed here some of the common reasons that teachers have offered for the study of literature. In our own experience as readers, we have delighted in encountering interesting characters, chuckled, reflected, and shuddered at biting satire, delighted in novel, graceful, and lyrical uses of language, lost track of time as we traveled with characters we cared about, learned much about worlds outside our own neighborhoods, grappled with complicated ideas and questions, and pondered human experience.

We acknowledge that all of these experiences and responses and more give us reason to read and teach literature. But for most adolescents, who want to feel competent in the skills that they value and connected to their peers, the inquiries into consequential, everyday problems invite them to devote the time and the cognitive energy into reading complex literary texts.

We suggest that as a beginning point, teachers of literature need to know darn well why they have studied literature and why they are asking students to study literature. We discourage teachers from trying to build a case before their students. Instead, we suggest an inquiry-driven leap into the compelling problems that some selected literature explores. This does not mean a narrow assignment of a problem or theme to a complex work of literature, as if *Romeo and Juliet* is simply about romantic love and *Hamlet* is simply about revenge. We have found that in following an inquiry path, our students are able to experience the range of joys in reading literature—the entertainment, the language, the thinking, the reflections. And if the problem at the core of the inquiry is a rich one, it will spark many questions and perhaps inspire the reading of many texts.

Of course, the study of literature is a discipline, and as such, the development of some advanced skills requires a sense of a worthwhile goal, demonstrations by someone who has some expertise, extensive practice, and dialogue with peers. In the previous chapter, we laid out an outline of a sequence for the teaching of literature in a high school. We contend that once a teacher has offered students a point of entry into a complex work of literature, the teacher has the obligation to show learners how a mature reader reads such a text closely and critically. The chapters that follow offer ways to initiate inquiry into literature, how to show adolescents how to read literature, how to foster dialogue about literary texts, and how to encourage an enthusiasm for reading.

YOUR VIEW

No doubt you have strong feelings about the value of reading literature, and these feelings have evolved over your life as a reader. With some of your peers, share your thoughts about why people read literature and why adolescents should study literature.

1. Not as a persuasive speech to convince adolescents to read, but as an affirmation of the value in your endeavor, explain to a peer why you think it is important to study literature and why adolescents should read some difficult texts that you have selected for them to read.
2. How can you make the study of literature an engaging and meaningful experience for a group of adolescents who may not share your enthusiasm for reading?

Chapter 3

Preparing for the Literature Experience

You can probably recall sitting at a meal with a group of acquaintances, with two or three members of the group sharing a story that obviously amuses them, while you and perhaps another member of the group looked on baffled. The point of the story and how it is amusing escaped you because you lacked the experience on which the story was based, failing to understand the references and why certain events befalling certain persons would be mirthful. Similarly, if you are an experienced auto mechanic, you might breeze through a technical report about an automotive recall, while someone who has never looked under the hood of a car might struggle to make sense of the language and the significance of the descriptions and warnings.

These experiences speak to basic elements of learning and reading: the more we know, the easier it is to learn more; the more we know about a subject, the easier it is to read about that subject. Even if the text poses some problems for us and if we are able to connect it to what we already know, we might be willing to struggle with the challenging text. In addition, the reading that baffles and frustrates us might make us feel incompetent, while the reading that we can accomplish with some facility because we can connect the content to experiences we have had or concepts we already know is likely to bring us delight or satisfaction.

Let's imagine Mr. Leibniz about to embark with his ninth graders on the reading of *A Tale of Two Cities*, a required text in the ninth-grade curriculum. Recognizing that his students probably know little about the French Revolution, the Reign of Terror, England's long history of conflict with France, and the life and work of Charles Dickens, Mr. Leibniz has prepared a lecture supported by carefully designed PowerPoint slides with embedded images, video clips, and sound bites.

Before beginning his presentation, Mr. Leibniz emphasized to his young scholars that they should be taking notes, which they would use to prepare for the next day's quiz on the content. Perhaps not surprisingly, the next day only a few students receive much higher than a passing grade on the quiz. A week into the reading of the novel, several students complain that they are having difficulty in following the narrative: "I can't keep the characters straight!" "How do you get 'recalled to life'?" "Why is Lucie going to Paris?" "Who is Jerry Cruncher?" "What's with all the shoe-making business?" Alas, poor Leibniz's efforts seemed for naught.

While Mr. Leibniz is clearly making some effort to ready the learners for reading the novel, he went about the preparation in the wrong way. Perhaps he failed on two counts: he attempted to *transmit* knowledge, and he delivered information that, even if committed to memory by all the students, would not actually help them to read the novel. What *would* actually help students to read a long, complex narrative?

If teachers are to ask students to read a text, especially a complex literary text, those teachers have an obligation to assess the extent to which the learners have sufficient knowledge and experience to be willing to read the text and be able to comprehend what they have made an effort to understand. The emergence of the Common Core State Standards has sparked many debates about the merits of pre-reading activities, with some CCSS champions advising the curtailment, if not the total elimination, of pre-reading activities in order to promote "productive struggle" with complex texts (Gewertz, 2012).

Reading educator Timothy Shanahan (2013) acknowledges some value in pre-reading, if done appropriately:

> Cognitive psychology has defined reading comprehension in terms of a reader's ability to integrate text information with prior knowledge to form a mental representation or memory. Thus, "close reading" of a text for which one lacks the necessary background information required to understand it may not be a very productive process for some learners. (7)

The concern of some CCSS advocates is that some pre-reading activities can supplant the actual reading of a text. As an example of a misguided frontloading effort, if the teacher engages learners in a pre-reading activity that helps learners to recognize signs of mental illness—including obsessive behavior, conflict with a parent, and distancing of oneself from friends and romantic interest—then students who encounter Hamlet are going to be inclined to judge him to be mad and see his madness as the cause of his downfall. At the same time, students who know little about czarist Russia, the Russian Revolution, the emergence of Joseph Stalin, and the purge trials under his rule are going to see little allegorical nuance in their reading of *Animal Farm*, if they see any allegory at all.

Again, a teacher's judgment about how and whether to design pre-reading activities for the reading of a narrative will depend much on knowing the text and seeing the demands it makes on a particular group of learners. Simply put, the teacher needs to know the learners and the text well. To call a text "complex" depends on the reader who will encounter that text. Decisions about the design and appropriateness of a pre-reading activity are a product of careful task analysis: that is, the teacher asks, "What do these learners need to know and need to be able to do in order to complete this task successfully?" In this case, *successfully* might mean reading a text "closely" and critically. And, what students *need to know* will depend on what they *already know*.

SOME DO'S AND DON'T'S

There are many occasions when teachers in middle school and high school will want to frontload the reading of a complex text. At the same time, there are good ways and bad ways to go about doing this. The guidelines below suggest some principles to keep in mind for designing pre-reading activities. The simple theme of these guidelines is that the pre-reading should enhance and not supplant the reading of a literary text. Shanahan (2013) offers a summary of the problem:

> Of course, one person's presupposed background information is another's plot summary. One group of researchers found that giving information ahead of time powerfully enhanced comprehension and recall. However, what they offered was an extensive preview that was repetitive of the text itself. (8)

So, as Shanahan reminds us, the goal is to *prepare* readers for reading a text and not enable them to avoid it. In Shanahan's (2013) caution, he sets the parameters: Preparing students to read a text is perfectly reasonable, and it's compatible with the Common Core State Standards. But such preparation should be brief and should focus on providing students with the tools they need to make sense of the text on their own. Some texts may require providing students with a context to minimize interpretive problems; with other texts, it might make more sense to *not* provide background but to carefully observe as students confront the information, querying them about the potentially confusing stuff and adding any necessary explanation before a second reading. (p. 10)

Teacher licensure candidates and experienced teachers have shared their observations, represented below as a set of guidelines. These guidelines appear below. The balance of this chapter provides examples of pre-reading activities that serve a variety of purposes and are consistent with these guidelines.

FEATURES OF A USEFUL PRE-READING ACTIVITY

Does the following:

Derives from a careful task analysis that requires

- Knowing who the learners are.
- Recognizing the challenges the specific group of learners might have with a text.
- Recognizing the broader instructional goals and connection between the specific text and the goals.

Motivates students to want to read by

- Giving students confidence that they can actually read the text because the pre-reading
  - Prepares students to recognize and/or figure out vocabulary.
  - Prepares learners for new syntax, structure, allusions, and historical and literacy references.
- Represents the reading as a valued-shared experience.
- Exposes conflicting views about the text: how to interpret it and how to value it.

Provides a point of entry into a challenging text by

- Representing a starting point for an experience with a text.
- Encouraging other possibilities for experiencing and responding to a text.

Raises critical questions as possible foci and points of inquiry for the reading by

- Honoring the critical tradition that surrounds the text.
- Representing the inquiry as areas of doubt rather than consensus understandings.
- Positioning the inquiry into a specific text as part of a larger shared inquiry.

Equips learners with a critical framework for judging characters and the text as a whole by

- Facilitating the expression of criteria or standards that become the basis for judgments (e.g., Is this a tragedy? Is the character justified? Can we consider the character a hero?).

Engages learners in making critical judgments and in expressing related arguments by

- Allowing the collision of adverse positions.
- Promoting the civil and rational expression of critical judgments.
- Exposing learners to a variety of perspectives and arguments.
- Testing the merits of students' thinking against opposition.
- Drawing from the distributed knowledge of a group.

Encourages reflection about how one arrives at a critical judgment by

- Fostering an awareness of inferencing and critical judgment processes that, with practice, have a reasonable potential to transfer to the work with a text.

Allows for some discussion to be student-led, thus

- Giving students a good deal of autonomy about who will lead, how to proceed, how to report, how to record, and so on.

Does not involve the following:

- Revealing the plot and spoiling the experience or effect.
- Narrowing critical judgment to focus on one aphoristic statement of theme.
- Allowing learners to actually avoid reading the text.
- Standing alone as a "fun" activity, with no apparent connection to other learning.

PURPOSE-DRIVEN DESIGN

Pre-reading activities can be as simple as an anticipation guide, or as complicated as an extended simulation role-playing game. They might take the form of a journal entry and follow-up discussion, a survey, discussion of a brief article, responses to an image or quotation, a case study analysis, or a simulation. In deciding the necessity for the pre-reading and the form it should take, a teacher needs to know students well and the target text well.

A rich variety of pre-reading activities can engage adolescents in inquiry and discussion, and many teachers have been eager to share what they have used successfully. The good news, then, is that a teacher does not have to invent every pre-reading activity, although it is good to know how to construct one, and we offer some guidance later in this chapter. References to several useful resources follow below. The balance of the chapter offers examples selected in part for their brevity.

Smagorinsky et al. (1987) share a variety of surveys, ranking activities, scenarios, and simulations. Johannessen (1992) shares a variety of activities, including a simulation that allows students, safely, to experience what combat troops experience in dangerous situations. Johannessen et al. (2009) provide several examples of pre-reading activities that ultimately prepare learners for writing about literature. Smith and Wilhelm (2010) share activities designed to help readers think deeply about the core literary elements of character, setting, point of view, and theme.

Smagorinsky et al. (2012) offer examples of collaborative writing activities that can involve students in constructing a narrative that is similar in genre and structure to the more complex text that the students are about to read. McCann (2014), McCann et al. (2015, 2018), and Smagorinsky (2018) all offer examples of rich pre-reading activities that integrate discussion, writing, and reading and position students to inquire into complex concepts represented in a body of literature.

A few examples of fairly simple pre-reading activities follow, chosen to illustrate the use of such activities to serve a variety of purposes. Table 3.1 offers a summary of possible purposes for pre-reading activities.

Tapping into Prior Knowledge

Several works of literature invite the reader to judge the administration of justice or the failures in honoring principles and spirit of justice. Anyone who has worked with adolescents will testify that they are quick to point out when others have acted unjustly, especially their teachers. It is clear then that they

Table 3.1 Purposes Served by Pre-reading Activities

Purpose	Sample Activity Structure
Build background knowledge	Reading, sharing, and discussing "informational" text; viewing and discussing a film
Activate prior knowledge	Surveys, scenarios, case studies, simulations
Foster empathic responses to characters	Case study or simulation; writing a vignette
Anticipate the structure of the narrative	Collaborative writing of a narrative or projection from the fragment of a narrative
Raise critical questions or pose interpretive problems	Surveys, case studies, scenarios, simulations
Learn procedures for analysis	Discussion of images and scenarios

have notions of what it means to be *just*. For many encounters with literature—for example, *Merchant of Venice, To Kill a Mockingbird, The Hate U Give, All American Boys*—it is useful to have in mind a fairly well-thought-out conception of justice. As the work of Michael Sandel (2009) and John Rawls (1971/1999) demonstrates, deciding what *justice* is and acting in *just* ways can be quite complicated.

The following sample survey is likely to generate lots of discussion in the classroom and position students for reading-related texts critically. A teacher would want to use of the survey in three stages: (1) Introduce the purpose for the survey and invite students to respond independently. (2) Collect the data from the survey by whatever means you have available (e.g., show of hands, clickers). The collection of the data can be tedious, so another option is to ask students to identify the statements that they reacted to most sharply. Another option would be to direct students into small groups to discuss the statements that they cared about the most. (3) As a whole class, discuss the statements that the students judge to be the most important.

WHAT IS *JUSTICE*?

Use the following numbers to indicate the degree of your agreement or disagreement with the following statements: 4 = strongly agree; 3 = agree; 2 = disagree; 1 = strongly disagree. Note any situations or principles that guided your judgment.

1. Justice means "an eye for an eye, a tooth for a tooth."
2. Everyone should get what he/she deserves.
3. Justice and revenge are more or less the same thing.
4. In determining justice, you have to consider the greatest good for the greatest number of people.
5. Securing justice for some people should never impinge on the rights and welfare of others.
6. The end justifies the means.
7. "Injustice anywhere is a threat to justice everywhere."
8. The silent witnessing of injustice contributes to the erosion of justice.
9. Justice involves the honoring of values that are right and decent.
10. Justice and the rigid compliance with the law are not the same thing.
11. A society cannot have *justice* without having *equality*.
12. *Justice* and *equity* should not be confused.
13. *Justice* means striving toward the common good.
14. A *just* society is one that protects individual rights and honors human dignity.

You can expect from the discussion that students will express some rules or criterion statements for defining justice. Some students have shared these principles:

- People should get what they deserve.
- People should be treated as equals, no matter how rich or poor they are.
- Revenge might serve justice, but it is most intended to hurt someone.
- The best thing for the majority isn't justice, if it leaves some people suffering.
- If you witness injustice and don't do anything about it, you are just part of the problem.

There is no answer key for the survey. Finding the "right" answer is not the point. Instead, students are tapping into knowledge they have individually and collectively to construct some criteria that they can use to judge the behavior of characters in a novel or play.

Applying Criteria

An alternative activity could either activate prior knowledge through a different means or allow for students to apply established criteria to individual situations. John Rawls (1971/1999) invites us to think about "justice as fairness," not that *justice* and *fairness* are synonymous, but that "it [justice as fairness] conveys the idea that the principles of justice are agreed to in an initial situation that is fair" (p. 11). In other words, in order to conceive of standards for justice, members of a society would have to establish those rules from a position in which no one is "advantaged or disadvantaged in the choice of principles by the outcome of natural choice or the contingency of social circumstances" (p. 11). Again, adolescents are quick to report what is *unfair*, so they must have some sense of a standard by which they can make this judgment. The instructional goal, especially for the sake of preparing a group for reading critically, is for the students to voice a reasonable set of standards.

Ninth graders as well as university students have worked with the scenarios, consistently resulting in lively discussions in small groups and in the class as a whole. The following instructional sequence is useful: (1) Read the first scenario aloud and discuss it with the whole class. If the teacher proceeds in a dialogic way (i.e., with no pre-specified answers in mind), several students will contribute and work together to refine something that sounds like a rule for *fairness*. This initial dialogue offers the model that students should follow as they proceed into small group discussion. (2) The students work in small groups to discuss the remaining scenarios, with the goal of listing any statements that they judge to be reasonable rules. The teacher should circulate the room and monitor these discussions to judge the functionality of each group and to encourage the recording of criterion statements. (3) The class as a whole discusses each scenario.

The end product is a list of guidelines that readers can refer to as they judge the situations and actions in a play or novel. We offer here a set of scenarios along with a composite discussion to illustrate a common exchange among students.

FAIRNESS SCENARIOS

1. Ten-year-old Bennie Fitz and his seven-year-old sister Honey rode together in the back of their parents' sedan on the way to visit their grandparents at their home 80 miles away. During the first 40 minutes of the drive, everyone listened to Honey's CD of "Barney's Favorite Show Tunes" on the car stereo. Bennie pleaded with his parents: "Can we please listen to my music now? We've been listening to that stupid Barney CD for the whole ride." His mother responded, "That's all right, Bennie. We'll listen to your music on the way home." Was Mrs. Fitz being fair? Explain.
2. Abel Walker was stricken with chicken pox and was forced to stay home from his fourth-grade class for five days. During his absence, the class voted on where they would like to go for the class picnic at the end of the year. When the votes were counted, it was decided that the class would visit Harvest Valley Forest Preserve for their picnic. The second choice was Beaubien Pond. The vote was twelve to eleven. If Abel had been there he would have voted for Beaubien Pond. Abel was disappointed and asked his teacher Mrs. McAnthony to allow the class to vote again, but she refused. She said, "The class has already decided. It wouldn't be fair to vote again after you've tried to influence the decision. You'll just have to live with the decision." Was Mrs. McAnthony being fair? Explain.
3. Twenty members of the senior class at Floodrock High School have been identified as gifted. They qualify for the gifted program because they have IQ scores higher than 125, and they each scored above the 90th percentile in reading and mathematics. One "gifted" activity this year was to transport the twenty students to Cape Girardeau, Missouri, to see a performance of the Latvian Modern Dance Ensemble. When the gifted students missed a day of school, they were excused from any tests or homework for that day. Betty Braumeier, a senior who was not included in the gifted program this year, said, "That is so unfair. If one group of students are excused, we should all be excused." Do you agree with Betty? Why, or why not?

4. Faith McNaulty is a retired dock worker and a widow. She and her husband sent their three children to parochial schools, for which they had to pay substantial tuition. Her children are now grown and living on their own. Mrs. McNaulty has never used the local public schools for any reason. Although she voted against a recent tax referendum to pay for an addition to the local public high school, the referendum passed. Mrs. McNaulty will now have to pay an additional one hundred dollars per year to support the public school. According to Mrs. McNulty, what principle of fairness has been violated? Do you agree with her? Explain.
5. Durwood Parker works as an admissions officer at Middle Border State University, where he sometimes has to make difficult decisions about which candidates will be admitted to the school. Last spring, he had to choose between two students who had almost identical academic records. One student would be a graduate of Shoreline High School, a rather famous suburban high school with a strong reputation. The other student would graduate from Metro Core High School, an inner-city school with a reputation for gang troubles, violence, and general discord. Mr. Parker selected the student from Shoreline High, figuring that a graduate of that institution would surely be a more productive contributor to the university. Has Mr. Parker been fair? Why, or why not?

Discussion about the scenarios can go a variety of ways, and since there are no pre-specified answers the scenario-based activity is a good one for a teacher to refine skills at facilitating discussions. The teacher's function is to listen attentively to each speaker, paraphrase often, and invite other participants to evaluate the contributions. The teacher should also be alert to the expression of rules and record the ones for which there is consensus. The following excerpt represents a typical exchange.

Mr. Thomas: Now that we have read the first scenario, how would you decide? Is Ms. Fitz being fair with her children?
Maria: I think she is doing everything she can to be fair. I mean, she is giving each child equal amount of time to listen to the music they prefer.
Mr. Thomas: So, fairness means that everyone has to have an equal amount of what gives them pleasure.
Nathan: Well, that's too broad. I mean, you can't guarantee that everyone gets equal amounts of everything all the time. In some cases, you have to earn what you get and some people deserve more than others.
Mr. Thomas: How do you mean? Can you give an example?
Nathan: I don't know. Let me think about that.
Mr. Thomas: All right. How about this situation? Here at the high school, the principal gets a reserved parking space next to the entrance to the school, while I

have to park across the street and sometimes cross through rain and snow with my book bag and all. I ask you—is that fair?

Cynthia: Well, it could be, because you could have been principal and got that parking spot. I don't think that they pick just anyone to be principal. She had to earn it. I don't know what they do to be principal, but she had to earn it some way.

Mr. Thomas: So you think I had the opportunity. No one systematically denied me the opportunity for that choice parking spot?

Cynthia: That's kinda it. Everyone has to have the opportunity to enjoy the things that they need.

The class appears to be stumbling along, but it is this grappling with ideas and finding the language to express ideas that immerses students in procedures for defining. This in turn prepares them for reading about more complicated narratives in which justice and fairness are issues or concepts that the author explores extensively, including the obvious *Merchant of Venice, The Tempest, Great Expectations, Things Fall Apart, The Outsiders,* or the other texts mentioned above. The framework that students develop is a product of their interaction and construction and not a transmitted set of rules from the teacher. The discussion about a concept that a tradition of scholarship affirms is a focus for the play or novel does not inhibit adolescent readers from discovering and evaluating other thematic elements and having their own personal response to the literature.

Fostering an Empathic Response

In the earlier example, Mr. Leibnitz's presentation is unlikely to prepare adolescent learners for their reading of *A Tale of Two Cities.* Beyond any need to know about eighteenth-century France or the life of Charles Dickens, readers need to reflect on the possibility that someone who has lived a life of dissipation and indifference would want to make some grand gesture to reclaim his life. Is it too much to ask that someone would make the ultimate sacrifice of surrendering his life in order to advance the happiness of someone he loves and longs to be with? In preparing learners for the reading of the novel, a teacher might choose the discussion of another case to encourage students to put themselves in the place of a character that faces a situation that is in some ways similar to the condition of the character in the novel.

If a teacher is considering the use of case study discussions, it is useful to keep a couple of broad guidelines in mind. It helps to construct a central character that has some commonalities with the adolescent learners: that is, the character is a young person, possibly a high school student; the problem is set in a school or extends from life in school; and the central character is someone about whom the students can care. The case below, "Reclamation and Renewal," is an example of such a case.

This case and similar cases have prompted extensive discussions that led to elaborated written responses that introduce a complex work of literature. In using the "Reclamation and Renewal" case, teachers might follow a sequence that is similar to the work with a set of scenarios. The obvious first step is to read the case narrative with students. It is helpful to have students write a letter of advice to the character Billy, but it is useful for students to talk a bit with partners before they attempt to write. After this two-step sequence—discussion and writing—some volunteers will be willing to share their letters. The shared letters are likely to invite some polite criticism about the quality of the advice.

If students do not question the advice, the teacher can prompt the learners to think further about the implications of their advice. Here are some examples: Is there any need for a "dramatic and significant" act to renew one's life? How realistic is it that it suddenly dawns on someone that life has been wasted and a dramatic reclamation is necessary? Knowing what we know about substance abuse and rehabilitation, how likely is it that Billy will follow through with his initial intentions and follow someone else's sympathetic advice? In the end, if we put ourselves in the place of Billy Edwards, what will he likely do?

CASE STUDY: "RECLAMATION AND RENEWAL"

When Billy Edwards was a senior at Floodrock High School, he received scholarship offers from several universities that were impressed by his brilliant academic record. He ranked third in his class, earned impressive College Board exam scores, and received many academic and extracurricular honors. In addition to being an accomplished student, Billy was a virtuoso clarinet player in Floodrock's distinguished Jazz Band. After reviewing his many options, Billy decided to enroll in Tulane University in New Orleans, Louisiana, because the legal drinking age in that state at the time was only eighteen.

Billy thoroughly enjoyed his freshman year at Tulane. He joined Alpha Chi Epsilon fraternity, reveled in Mardi Gras, experienced frequent drinking binges, and generally neglected his studies. When Billy returned home after his freshman year, his family noticed distinct physical and attitudinal changes. He seemed to have lost all ambition. He stayed up well beyond midnight every night, and slept most days until noon. His physical appearance was startlingly unkempt, with a scruffy beard, wrinkled clothes, and distinctive body odor. And he was surly, taking almost violent offense at any constructive criticism or encouragement. While he was once very popular, he now had only a handful of the most disreputable associates.

Although Billy lost his academic scholarship, and he remained on academic probation, he was able to continue at Tulane. Billy's return to school came almost as a relief for his family, who suffered through the tension and volatility of Billy's presence. Billy soon turned to the use of drugs—first marijuana and hashish; then amphetamines and cocaine. Billy acted recklessly in many ways, including driving under the influence of drugs and alcohol as he roamed various parts of New Orleans and southern Louisiana. Although Billy seemed to survive each day in a stupor, he was bright enough to earn grades good enough to keep him in school, and he eventually graduated with a degree in philosophy.

After graduation, Billy took stock of himself. He realized that he had wasted much of his time, money, and talent during his four years of college. While he enjoyed brief and transitory physical pleasures, he accomplished almost nothing. He neglected to devote a brilliant mind to learn a subject and to extend the field of knowledge in his major. He neglected a significant musical talent. He neglected many friends, who quickly abandoned him. He neglected a family who loved him and had great hopes for his future. In general, he disappointed everyone, and ended up disgusting himself.

Billy is now quite despondent about his condition. His health has declined, his musical skills have atrophied, and his mind has suffered under chemical dependency. But Billy would like to *reclaim his life* somehow. He fears, however, that reclamation is almost impossible, because he has alienated his family, friends, and associates. Billy is bright enough to recognize that any reclaiming of his life will be a long process. In the meantime, he seeks to do *something dramatic* and *significant* to signal to others and affirm for himself that he has chosen a new path. He seeks advice, and a letter from you could provide some impetus and direction for his renewal. After talking to a group of your classmates about Billy's situation and goal, write a brief letter to Billy to explain what he needs to do to show others and to prove to himself that he is earnest in his intentions to return to the kind of person who showed such great promise at Floodrock High School four years ago.

The discussions of the Billy Edwards case served as one element in the preparation for the teaching of *A Tale of Two Cities*. Students were eager to discuss the situation and many members of the class were convinced that the narrative was a fictionalized version of someone they knew, even members of their own families.

Experiencing the Challenges and Arguments of the Narrative

Another pre-reading possibility is a simple simulation that demonstrates a problem and invites critical thought. The occasion is the reading of *Flowers for Algernon* with ninth graders, many of whom were in the "lower track" English class because they had been measured as performing two or more years below their grade level in reading. That is to say, psychometricians had devised a paper-and-pencil test that was intended to measure the learners' facility with reading, and decision-makers in the school used the results of the test to sort young people and assign them to specific classes deemed appropriate for their abilities.

One of the concepts that Charlie and some of the scientists depicted in the narrative struggle with is how to define *intelligence*. An operational and circular definition is that intelligence is whatever an intelligence test measures. So, what does such a test measure? The assumption is that an IQ test will present questions that any intelligent person should be able to answer correctly. Perhaps our IQs are limited, but we scratch our heads when we puzzle through this circular path, and students puzzle over this, too, especially when someone's test will be used to label and place them.

This occasion seemed the appropriate time for a simulation, with students in the position of a test-maker who works in teams to construct a kind of IQ test. All teams received these directions: "Write three multiple choice questions that you think any intelligent person should be able to answer. Provide three choices for each item and supply what you think is the correct answer to each question." The idea is for each of six or seven teams to generate three questions and their choices and then to pool the questions across all the teams.

In this situation, students readily generate questions. Some are sports and pop culture trivia, some are questions from the class they just had in the previous period, and some are bits of information they recall from their earlier school experience. The questions and choices require a bit of editing, but by and large the questions and choices should remain as submitted. A bit of clerical work for the teacher, then, is to type, format, and duplicate the test for administration in the next class meeting.

Students should have a fairly tight time limit in completing the test. The teacher can display the committees' answers, and the class can score the test themselves. With a laptop with a spreadsheet or simply a calculator on your phone, it is possible to quickly calculate the mean and the standard deviation for the results of the test. Since this is just a simulation, and no one has to see anyone else's score, a teacher might label the spread of scores: within −1 and +1 standard deviations means *average*; above +1 standard deviation means *above average*; below −1 standard deviation means *below average* or "struggling." The question for writing and discussing is this: If this test is representative of what IQ tests are like, *how accurate* are they for reporting your intelligence and *labeling* you?

Students are quick to talk about the limitations of the test and their skepticism about IQ tests generally as a way to sort and label learners. Students point out that the test items assume that recall of trivia is a mark of intelligence, that some questions are worded ambiguously, and that some of the presumed correct answers were just wrong. In our experience, students also questioned language that would label them as "struggling" or even "above average" when the test was insufficient for supporting such conclusions. Students also point out that the test defined *intelligence* in a very narrow way and did not take into account that intelligence could manifest itself in artistic, musical, or even social expressions.

This rather simple simulation positioned students to think critically about recurring issues in the novel: how we define intelligence, how we label and sort people based on some assessment of their intelligence, and how we judge the value of a person based in the perception of that person's intelligence. In turn, the experience helped students to reflect on the inadequacies in a system that measured, labeled, and sorted them.

Practicing the Procedures for Interpretation

Perhaps the most challenging task in reading literature is the recognition and interpretation of irony. After all, to interpret irony, the reader assumes the bold position of saying that regardless of what a text appears to be saying, the author probably intended the reader to see the opposite, or at least something different than the literal meaning. Wayne Booth observes that recognizing ironic tone is an essential in reading or listening: "every reader learns that some statements cannot be understood without rejecting what they seem to say" (1). Much is at stake when judging whether or not a text or statement is ironic. How do listeners know whether a politician's apparently racist tweet should be read as a bit of satire or taken quite literally? Should we read Machiavelli's *The Prince* as satire or as a literal guidebook for leadership? Then, of course, can we see ironies that the author failed to see or appreciate? And how do we explain to someone else how we saw signals within a text that allowed us to read it as ironic?

Some work with ironic texts offers examples of how a teacher can help learners to become aware of the *procedures* that mature readers follow in interpreting complex texts. A problem with irony, with sarcasm being perhaps the most common form among adolescents, is that we might sense it immediately while having some difficulty in explaining to others how we arrived at our judgment. It is like explaining how a joke is funny. But in arguing for an interpretation of a text as ironic or satirical, it is critical to be able to identify the features of the text and our knowledge about how to read ironic texts to say that something is ironic.

As a beginning point, it is useful to use a visual image to slow down the reading process and require that students point to specific details and explain how they can reject "what they seem to say," as Booth suggests. The example image here is a famous drawing from George Grosz (figure 3.1). The dialogue bubble says "KV," which abbreviates *kriegsverwendungsfähig*, perhaps the equivalent of OK, and usually translated as "Fit for Active Service," which becomes the title. It will be necessary to share this bit of information with students and the fact that the drawing was produced in Germany near the end of World War I. The following composite dialogue reveals what typically happens in discussion about the drawing.

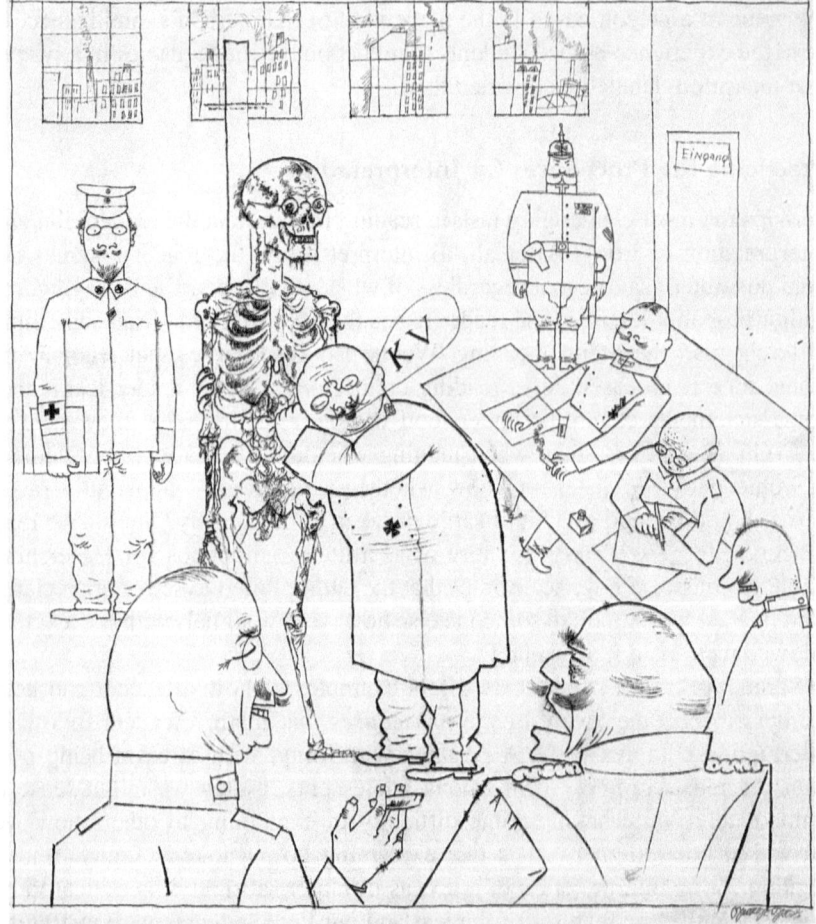

Figure 3.1 George Grosz. "Fit for Active Service." *Source:* George Grosz's drawing "Fit for Active Service" is reprinted by permission of the Museum of Modern Art, New York, New York.

Mr. Thomas: When I see this drawing, it tells me that at the end of World War I, the Germans were approving skeletons or cadavers to enter into military service. If I am wrong about that, how do you know?
Celia: Because that's impossible.
Mr. Thomas: But that's what the picture shows.
Celia: Yeah, but you know that's not possible, so you know that the artist meant something else.
Mr. Thomas: Okay. I guess that's our first clue. What do you expect when a draft board is selecting people to serve in the military?
Bobby: Well, you want guys who are strong or healthy at least, if they are going to fight. And this is the opposite.
Mr. Thomas: So, you notice that the situation is the opposite of what you would normally expect. What else do you notice in the picture?
Barbara: The men sitting around the table are like kinda chubby, like well-fed. And some of them are laughing.
Mr. Thomas: Yeah?
Barbara: It's not funny. They are sending someone off to war. That's serious.
Mr. Thomas: So we have another opposite.

And so the process continues with this drawing or other illustrations, like the kind often found on the cover of the *New Yorker* or other magazines. Several students will be inclined to jump right away to an interpretation. It is important to slow down and deconstruct the image to say explicitly how the interpretation is derived. Such discussions lead to a preliminary set of "rules" for reading irony. There are contrasts or contradictions. The image shows a situation that is the opposite of what we would normally expect. Things are exaggerated.

From this point, a teacher could move on to a series of constructed texts. As a rule, these brief narratives should be set in a school and depict situations that the high school students can well imagine. Again, as with the earlier set of scenarios, it is helpful to model the discussion by working as a whole class on the first situation; then students can work in small groups to read the remaining texts and discuss them with the object to derive a set of "rules" for reading irony. Some sample texts appear below. Students readily discuss these little narratives, but teachers can also construct similar ones that they think will resonate with their particular learners.

WHAT DOES THE SPEAKER REALLY MEAN?

Directions: For each of the following descriptions, answer the accompanying questions. Be prepared to explain to the rest of the class the process a reader should follow in order to determine the "true" meaning that the speaker hoped to express or that the situation reveals.

1. When I opened up the ice chest at the picnic, there were about a million cans of beer and not a single diet soda. As usual, my thoughtful father remembered to bring beverages for himself and nothing for my mother and me.
   a. What does the narrator really think about her father?
   b. How do you know her true feelings?
2. You can imagine how overjoyed I was to learn that I had failed my exam, the second quarter, and the semester. In fact, my grade was the lowest score on the calculus final. My parents are going to be thrilled about this. My future sure looks rosy.
   a. How does the speaker really feel about his grades?
   b. How do you know how the speaker really feels?
3. One thing that Harriet liked about Robert was his leather jacket. One thing Robert liked about Harriet was her braided gold chain. At Christmas, Harriet wanted to please Robert, and Robert wanted to please Harriet; however, they were both short of cash. Robert decided to sell his leather jacket in order to buy Harriet the locket she wanted for her chain. Harriet, for her part, decided to sell her gold chain in order to get enough money to buy Robert some expensive leather gloves that would match his jacket exactly.
   a. How do Harriet and Robert want the other to feel about the present each has selected?
   b. How will they really feel about the present they receive?
4. Billy's mother likes to experiment with her cooking. In the past year, she has served Billy beef tongue with prune sauce, fried turkey livers with dill gravy, chili-rice krispie pie, and caviar paste mousse with spring vegetables. On Thursday evening when Billy arrived home late from basketball practice, he sat down at the dinner table, and his mom served him creamed catfish whiskers on a bed of shredded lettuce. When Billy's mother asked how him how he liked the dinner, he replied, "It's interesting."
   a. What does Billy really think about the dinner his mother serves him?
   b. How do you know how Billy really feels?
5. Mr. Boynton's fifth period pre-algebra class has been very unruly all year. There have been several fights in class. Class is often disrupted when books, paper airplanes, spitballs, and other projectiles have been hurled across the room. On one day, someone set fire to the projection screen. The class, however, seemed interested in having Mr. Boynton like them. One day toward the end of the year, one girl asked, "Mr.

Boynton, are we your favorite class?" Mr. Boynton said, "Well, this is a very unique class. I can't remember ever having a class quite like this one. How could you not be one of my favorites?"
a. What does Mr. Boynton really think about his class?
b. How do you know what Mr. Boynton thinks?

The discussion about these simple situations allows students to become aware of how they detect irony. That means they are aware of some procedures for analysis. In discussing the Grosz drawing and the constructed texts, students typically offer these features of the text that serve as clues that the speaker or artist is working in an ironic spirit:

- The speaker exaggerates by overstating.
- The speaker exaggerates by understating.
- The situation is the opposite of what you would normally expect.
- There is a contrast or contradiction.
- The speaker says something that is obviously untrue, and it appears that the speaker appreciates that the audience would know it to be untrue.

This is not an answer key; these are just some of the statements that classes have constructed through discussion. Readers might want to consult Wayne Booth's *A Rhetoric of Irony* and Michael W. Smith's *Understanding Unreliable Narrators* for more extensive discussion of textual clues and readers' procedures for recognizing and interpreting irony. As introductory activities to prepare students for reading selected complex texts, these examples emphasize how the pre-reading can help learners to be aware of specific *procedures* for reading.

DESIGN PRINCIPLES

This chapter offers a few possibilities for helping students to find a point of entry into a complex text and equipping them with some tools for interpretation. Perhaps most powerfully, a well-designed pre-reading activity offers a gateway into a rich literary text by raising questions and interpretive problems that engage readers in exploring texts and preparing them to discuss the texts meaningfully with others. In other words, the preparation can position learners to be actively involved in working with a text. Consider this general encouragement:

> in preparing younger readers for their encounters with some difficult texts, an English teacher would need to know how to design pre-reading activities that

introduce critical questions and prepare learners with the interpretive tools to be able to recognize and trace patterns, deconstruct symbols, and reflect on the questions that an author raises. (McCann and Knapp, 2019, p. 43)

Earlier in this chapter, a summary chart lists some "do's and don'ts" for designing pre-reading activities. While there are several resources for pre-reading activities that teachers have already designed, we understand that teachers will want to design their own activities to serve a particular group of learners as they approach a particular text or set of texts. Sometimes such activities allow students to define an abstract concept, sometimes the activity fosters an empathic response to characters, sometimes the activity raises critical questions or poses an interpretive problem, and sometimes the activity involves learners in the procedures for interpretation. Even with such variety of possibilities, there are some general principles of design, which appear below.

PRINCIPLES OF DESIGN FOR PRE-READING ACTIVITIES

1. Identify the *target outcome* by expressing what you would like learners to be able to do as a result of their learning. This step requires *envisioning* what achievement of the target outcome looks like.
2. Complete a *task analysis* of the anticipated reading, considering the characteristics of the learners and the complexities of the text: What do the learners need to know? What do they need to be able to do?
3. Through reflection and informal assessment, gauge the learners' *prior knowledge* and *interests*, relative to the target outcome.
4. Formulate an *appropriate problem* that taps prior knowledge and interests and will engage the learners in the relevant processes that can transfer to new learning.
5. Provide some *data* (e.g., an image, a survey, scenarios, a case, etc.) to which students can react.
6. Structure a *small group task* that has the following features: a specific goal, an opportunity for all learners to participate, a time limit, a dynamic that prompts interaction, and an expectation for sharing with the larger group.
7. Plan for *summarizing the activities* and for highlighting the agreements, commitments, or general conclusions of the group.
8. Provide for the *transition* from the set of preparatory activities to the subsequent learning, by explicitly noting connections and by explaining how procedures apply to a product, a task, or a performance.

9. Build in a *self-reflection* component that encourages the learners to be consciously aware of the procedures they followed in order to investigate a problem, formulate conclusions, and complete a product or performance.

YOUR VIEW

This chapter makes a case for using pre-reading activities to prepare students for their encounters with complex texts, and we offer some examples of inquiry- and discussion-based activities. You might have some reservations about using the kind of activities that we feature in this chapter, or you might think of other possibilities outside our limited repertoire. With some of your peers, discuss your thoughts about the value and the possibilities for pre-reading activities.

1. To what extent do you judge the use of pre-reading activities are an important part of teaching students to read literature?
2. Consider a particular text that you will be introducing to students. How could you prepare them, either by using one of the types of activities featured in this chapter or another kind of your own design?

Chapter 4

Noticing and Making Meaning

As we have shared in chapter 1, we owe much to Peter Rabinowitz to help us think about the discipline of reading narratives. Rabinowitz (1987) and Rabinowitz and Smith (1998) identify categories of rules for an authorial reading of a text. Our intention is to suggest to teachers how to help learners discover those rules, at least in students' own rudimentary terms, and practice applying those rules as part of a process of analysis and evaluation of literature. Consider Benjamin Bloom's reliable observation that if you want students to do something, like read a complex work of literature carefully and critically, you need to show them how to do it.

This chapter and the two that follow suggest two basic pedagogical sequences: (1) meet students where they are and then move from the simple and familiar to the more complex and unfamiliar; (2) with students' contributions, model processes for critical reading and then structure and monitor practice with the procedures. In contrast to a pronounced reader response stance, consider what Rabinowitz and Smith (1998) call an *authorial reading*. This means that the reader begins by asking what the author probably expected the intended audience to recognize. This position respects that the author made conscious decisions in the construction of the text.

There is much that a reader can discover that the author was perhaps unaware of, or about which the author might say she or he never intended. Perhaps the process of reading literature is in itself a creative act, but teachers should resist allowing words to mean anything a reader wants them to mean or at indulging in associations and reflections that move readers far away from the original text. Any reader's experience with a work of literature will be a personal response, but that response builds on a disciplined effort to understand what an author expected us to recognize and to apply rules from language and tradition to construct meaning by attending to the features of the text and connecting these features to what we already know. You'll find, then, in this chapter, some suggestions for getting started with a narrative image from popular culture and then expanding to a relatively simple, conventional text.

GETTING STARTED

It is first period at Gompers East High School, and after noting the purpose for the current lesson and its connection to what the students have been discussing, Ms. Jeffries projects a drawing (see Figure 4.1) from a *New Yorker* magazine cover. As with many of the covers of the *New Yorker*, the drawing suggests a narrative, one that is implicative both in the story's development and its tone. Ms. Jeffries introduces the drawing in this way:

> I saw this picture on the cover of the magazine and it told me a story. At first the story was pretty simple. But each time I look at the drawing, I get a different impression. I'm curious to know what you think, especially since this might relate to what we will be reading. But I want to try something a bit different. Before you start telling me the story as you see it, I would like you to point out some of the things you think the artist expected the reader to notice, especially the reader of *New Yorker* magazine. To begin, I should note that the title of the drawing is "Stop."

Most students in the class can see the projected image quite well, but Ms. Jeffries provides printed copies for a couple of students who request them. As discussed in chapter 3, in planning for the lesson, Ms. Jeffries would have to reflect on the prior knowledge students might need to be able to interpret the image. Would students recognize the urban landscape? Is the vehicle at the center of the frame obviously a police cruiser? Would this information likely emerge during discussion? Can students grapple with their construction of meaning from the image without this knowledge?

Ms. Jeffries decided that the image is accessible enough for most viewers that she would not need to frontload their discussion by noting the location or by identifying the vehicle as a police car, perhaps even a Chicago police cruiser. Some students or the teacher will likely point this information out as discussion develops, and students will have much to say about the picture even without knowledge about urban neighborhoods or Chicago police.

The instructional sequence begins with a whole class discussion about the features that students notice in the drawing. This interchange will allow the class to identify some general rules for reading a picture, especially one that suggests a narrative. By extension, the noting of elements in the picture will allow the class to generalize about rules for noticing features of a written narrative. As the lesson continues, the students work in small groups to discuss the meaning that they derive from the picture.

Ms. Jeffries: You have had a few minutes to look at this picture. So, what do you think the artist wanted the viewer to notice?
Antonia: Kids are walking to school, and a couple of cops are watching them.
Ms. Jeffries: You noticed that there is a police car and two officers in the middle of the picture.

Figure 4.1. "Stop" by Chris Ware. *Source:* Chris Ware's drawing "Stop," March 14, 2016, *The New Yorker*, reprinted by permission of Chris Ware.

Benjamin: But the cops aren't actually looking at the kids. They are looking to the side, like they are on patrol looking for something, expecting something bad to happen.

Ms. Jeffries: Thanks, Benjamin. So, you are noticing a couple of important characters and what they seem to be doing.

Celia: There's like a crossing guard in the middle of the picture.

Lawrence: She is holding up a stop sign, and the title of the picture is "Stop." And she is standing in front of the cop car.

Ms. Jeffries: So, you notice a central character and where she is positioned to bring her to our attention.

Celia: She is standing between the cop car and the little kids crossing the street. You would think that the cops would know to stop to let the kids pass, but she is like protecting the little kids from the cops.

Jarius: You have to protect them from the police.

Ms. Jeffries: Perhaps we are getting a bit ahead of ourselves, if we are just pointing out what the artist probably expected us to notice.

Allison: The police are supposed to protect everyone. In the picture, the cops are these two big white guys. The one on the left looks like he is wearing a bulletproof vest. And the car is really big, like a big SUV, so they probably can't even see the kids over the hood.

Jarius: It's like the kids are invisible to the cops, and if it wasn't for the crossing guard there, the cops could run over the kids.

Ms. Jeffries: So, you think that the artist figured we would notice that the cops are looking away and couldn't even see the kids if they were looking straight ahead.

Allison: Yeah. That is obvious. And it is just a woman crossing guard, unarmed and everything, who stands between the big cop car and the kids.

Ms. Jeffries: As you look elsewhere in the drawing, what else do you notice?

Fernando: The woman is looking straight down at the kids, like watching over them. She is the one who is watching out for them, protecting them.

Jimmy: You got to go back to the title. It says, "Stop." The crossing guard stands between the kids and the cops and holds up a sign for the cops to stop. That's like the opposite of the way it is supposed to be. It should be the cops who are watching out for the kids and protecting them.

Jarius: No one wants to say the obvious: the cops are white and the kids are black. It looks like everyone else in the neighborhood is black.

Ms. Jeffries: OK. Now we are getting into the meaning you are getting out of the picture. Let me add an observation of my own. It looks like it is winter. There is no greenery. You can see a few bare tree limbs in the background. I don't know if that matters, but I think the artist intended to offer a kind of barren landscape.

Antonia: Hmm. I'm not sure what to make of that. But you know it is not like a suburban community with a big lawn and trees in front of the school. There is litter on the street, and everything is like brick and pavement and sidewalks. It is kinda sad.

Ms. Jeffries: We focused most of our attention on the figures in the foreground, so, as a rule, we ought to pay close attention to the "major characters": in this case, the ones at the center in the foreground. And we should especially note their physical features and their gestures, particularly when there is no dialogue.

SMALL GROUP DIALOGUE

The brief exchange above is rudimentary. Ms. Jeffries meant the activity as a way to slow down the process of reading a narrative to help the students to become aware of what they notice and what they think the author expected them to notice. So far, in this example, the class has been noting distinctive features of the drawing. The next step is for the students to assign some meaning to what they see.

Ms. Jeffries put the learners into small groups (mostly groups of four), not randomly, but by keeping in mind the specific characteristics of the learners so that there is reasonable hope of having divergent opinions within the group and otherwise marginalized learners will have a good chance of being included in the discussions. Here is the prompt that initiated the discussions in the small groups: *Given the features that the artist probably expected an audience to notice from the picture, what do you think the artist/author expected an audience to conclude? Is this drawing a celebration of the way that adults protect children in a community? Is the drawing a critical statement about the need to protect young people from the police? Is it something else?*

The following example is a composite of many small groups. This one involves four students.

Rey: The first thing, like in bright red in the middle of the picture, is the stop sign the woman is holding. And the title is "Stop." So, like, the painter wanted to emphasize that word.

Sylvia: That sounds good. But the crossing guard is holding the sign up high for the cops to see. No one else is in the street to stop.

Thomas: Yeah, the woman is the crossing *guard*, and she is guarding the little kids. When she stands in front of the cop car, it is like she is guarding the kids from the cops.

Layla: But that doesn't mean that the artist is saying that the cops are a threat to the kids. The cops are looking around, like they are looking out for trouble on the sidewalks while the woman looks at the kids in the street. They are like working together to protect everyone in the neighborhood.

Thomas: As somebody said, the cop car is huge, compared to the little kids. The kids don't even come up to the hood. The cops are like big and powerful and the kids are tiny and vulnerable.

Layla: If the cops don't pay attention or don't see the kids, they could roll right over them.

Thomas: Or the artist is saying that young Black people could easily be destroyed by the white cops. The kids are like invisible, like they are nothing to the cops.

Sylvia: I like what Thomas is saying. But the magazine is from 2016. That's before all the protests and everything.

Thomas: This stuff has been going on for a long time, not just with George Floyd.

This is a small part of a larger exchange, yet much is happening as the students talk about what they notice and the meaning they construct from what they notice. As the lesson progresses, perhaps into a second day, the class participates in a whole group discussion to share their interpretations of the drawing. As a facilitator of the large group discussion and the monitor of the small group interchanges, the teacher can note the procedures that the students followed as they noticed details from the drawing and constructed meaning by connecting these details to what they already knew about human behavior, societal agents and expectations, current events, contrasts in setting, and narrative structure. One targeted result from the three discussions is that the teacher can highlight the "rules" that the learners applied to their viewing and interpreting. Here, then, are the general procedures that Ms. Jeffries constructed with the input of her students and shared with the class for them to confirm and note:

MS. JEFFRIES' CLASS'S RULES OF NOTICE

- The title has a privileged place, and the reader should interrogate its possible meaning and reflect on its implications as the story progresses.
- The reader should notice which characters are in the "foreground" of the story and note how the author has depicted them—for example, their ages, their physical features, their dress, their gestures, their relationship to each other.
- The reader should notice any secondary characters, and should be especially attentive to characters who might represent a contrast with another.
- The reader should notice any signs and symbols, especially those that might have a connection with the title of the story.
- The reader should notice the setting of the story—both the immediate surroundings and the placement within a larger environment.
- The reader should notice the vantage point for viewing the characters and action of the narrative.

In addition to noting what an author might expect an audience to notice, Ms. Jeffries's class also drew from their experience as readers of literature to apply *rules of signification*. In this context, this means they intuitively applied rules to interpret gesture, position, proximity, and symbols. The students pointed out that the crossing guard stands between two patrolmen who are supposed to "serve and protect" and the small children that the officers probably could not see over the car hood. They saw that the crossing guard is dressed in yellow and holds a read sign, with the hot colors contrasting with the cooler or neutral colors that dominate the scene.

Even if the students were not familiar with urban scenes of police cruising a neighborhood, they could see the contrast between the light-skinned police officers and the darker-skinned residents of the neighborhood. They knew that an event in the news suggested a connection to the scene. Essentially, Black Lives Matter protests sought reform to police perceptions and tactics that made young black people targets for excessive force. The students also attached meaning to the fact that a single black woman was demanding that the police *stop*.

While rules of signification are complex and shifting, Ms. Jeffries's class noted a few that could serve them as they move forward in reading more conventional printed texts. The summary below offers some rules that represent a starting point in interpreting the key features of a narrative.

MS. JEFFRIES' CLASS'S RULES OF SIGNIFICATION

- Gestures have meaning based on tradition and experience.
- The placement of characters and their depiction influence whether or not we sympathize with them.
- Contrasts and contradictions raise questions and invite resolution.
- Actions influence further actions, which allow us to account for the current state and predict future events.
- Symbols, including images, have meaning suggested by tradition and conventions within a culture.

Application and Practice with Rules

Of course, the interpretation and assessment of literature is far more complicated than the application of a few rules derives from talking about a picture. The two lists above are just a starting point, and students will not necessarily have a command of these procedures without substantial practice with them.

Experience suggests two key instructional practices: (1) Students need to work with each other in interpreting a relatively simple text to *derive* and express the "rules" or procedures that they apply in constructing meaning for a narrative. Although students may have been applying rules of notice and signification for as long as they have been readers, they need to be consciously aware of the procedures they and their peers have been employing. (2) Students need *substantial practice* in applying the rules they have derived and in expanding on the rudimentary set of rules they have initially identified. In discussing narratives and writing about narratives, students come to rely on the rules they have discovered, especially the rules of signification, to serve as warrants that allow them to attach meaning to the elements of the story that they have noticed and to the pattern of elements that they can identify.

In the instructional sequence described in this chapter, students can transfer the procedures for noticing and for constructing meaning about a picture to their subsequent reading of a relatively simple short story. For illustration, consider Gary Soto's often anthologized story "Like Mexicans." A few passages appear in this chapter, but the entire story is reproduced as an appendix. The example here illustrates some rudimentary moves in noticing and reflecting on elements of the story.

A discussion of the story follows in greater depth in chapter 5. Again, as discussed in chapter 3, a teacher will want to consider the elements of the story that might pose some difficulties for a particular group of readers. In this case, the central conflict and the themes of the story probably will not require much foregrounding for most adolescents. Some vocabulary, however, might be unfamiliar to some students, but these words and expressions can be easily glossed as the class begins reading and discussing the story.

As a beginning point in practicing with rules of notice and rules of signification, we propose a three-step sequence. First, following a read aloud/think aloud protocol, the teacher demonstrates a process of active reading. Instead of reading quickly and fluently, the teacher reads in a rather halting way, because she pauses from time to time to report what she notices, the questions she ponders, the expectations she has, the connections she makes, and so on. In other words, she is modeling in a rather slow-motion fashion the procedures that an experienced reader of literature would apply to the text.

The next step is for the teacher to call on a couple of brave souls in the class to continue to read aloud and imitate the teacher in "thinking aloud" as the reader progresses through the text. It is not a good idea to read the whole short story in this way, unless the story is very short. Instead, after a couple of students have taken a turn, the teacher can organize the class into pairs or into small groups to finish the reading of the story through a read aloud/think aloud protocol.

A teacher and a class would not want to practice this laborious way of reading as a regular routine. But such a way of reading and thinking out loud demonstrates and highlights procedures that the learners can employ during their more independent efforts and during discussions of texts. Here, then, is Ms. Jeffries in action as she shares her reading of the story.

Ms. Jeffries: As I said, I am going to begin reading the story "Like Mexicans" aloud for a little while. My intention is to use the sets of rules you constructed and apply them to thinking about the story. I don't want to do all of the work, so I will call on a couple of you to read a little bit in the way that I have. You'll have time with a partner to finish reading the story. Then we will have a chance to talk about what you think about the story. So, here goes. Right away the title "Like Mexicans" makes me pause. The author titled the story in this way for some reason. I do recall reading somewhere that Gary Soto is Mexican-American. So he is comparing some other people to Mexicans. Maybe he has met some non-Mexicans whom he doesn't know and he has to figure out something about their identities. Can anyone else think of some other possibilities?

Natalie: I guess the other possibility is that he *likes* Mexicans. He is not comparing. He is just saying that he likes them.

Ms. Jeffries: That could be a possibility. I'll have to keep the title in mind as I progress. Let's begin the story itself. "My grandmother gave me bad advice and good advice when I was in my early teens. For the bad advice, she said that I should become a barber because they made good money and listened to the radio all day. 'Honey, they don't work como burros,' she would say every time I visited her. She made the sound of donkeys braying. 'Like that, honey!' For the good advice, she said that I should marry a Mexican girl." This makes me think about my grandfather and my parents. Sometimes they offered advice that seemed pretty narrow-minded, based on their own experience and narrow view of things. But they offered advice to protect me and help me. I notice that Gary seems to be the first character in the story, and he is telling the story about himself. So this is probably his recalling some actual experiences with his grandmother. Does anyone else notice anything, especially based on our "rules"?

Gilbert: They sort of speak Spanish. Not always. I think that the grandmother was the one who came from Mexico, so we are supposed to notice that she is like the old-fashioned one.

Ms. Jeffries: So the grandmother goes on with her advice: "'No Okies, hijo'—she would say—'Look my son. He marry one, and they fight every day about I don't know what and I don't know what.' For her, everyone who wasn't Mexican, black, or Asian was an Okie. The French were Okies; the Italians in suits were Okies." So, here, at the opening of the story, the grandmother warns Gary to marry only a Mexican, and everyone non-Mexican, black, or Asian falls into her category of "Okies." I know that's an old term for people from the Plains states, including Oklahoma, who went to California looking for a better life during the Great Depression and the Dust Bowl. I think Gary, the author, expects us to notice that his grandmother is older and not particularly sensitive. Does anyone else notice anything?

Layla: She is telling him that he should marry a Mexican, so you can expect that he is going to like someone who is not Mexican. So his grandmother is probably going to be mad.

Derrick: And the title of the story.

Ms. Jeffries: What about it?

Derrick: He probably likes someone who is "like Mexicans" but not really Mexican.

Ms. Jeffries: That seems like a reasonable guess. OK, let me just finish this paragraph. "When I asked about Jews, whom I had read about, she asked for a picture. I rode home on my bicycle and returned with a calendar depicting the important races of the world, 'Pues si, son Okies tambien!' she said, nodding her head. She waved the calendar away, and we went to the living room where she lectured me on the virtues of the Mexican girl: first, she could cook, and second, she acted like a woman, not a man, in her husband's home. She said she would tell me about a third when I got a little older." First, I notice that they are at the grandmother's house, because he rides home to get a book. It also seems very important to him to learn who is an Okie and who is not. I also notice that the grandmother has some strong prejudices, but it's not uncommon for parents to want their kids to marry someone similar to them, to the parents. That's a shame and very narrow-minded, but probably true.

Veronica: My grandfather said that his mother drove with his uncles down to his college to break up the relationship he had with a girl in college because she was not Greek. So, that's my great-grandmother. She already had picked out a nice Greek girl for my grandfather. He didn't like her, though.

Ms. Jeffries: So I guess Gary expected us to notice this form of prejudice and recognize that it is pretty common. Could I get someone else to read the next paragraph? But not fast. I need you to read the way I did, perhaps pausing at the end of each sentence or whenever you notice something you think the author wanted us to recognize.

This process could continue for a couple of more paragraphs. Ideally, students will contribute, and with students' help, the teacher is modeling a process of active reading, drawing upon the rules of notice that the class as a whole had derived. It is not necessary to continue the demonstration for long. For some students in some classes, it will be a bit of a revelation to see a mature reader engaged slowly in procedures for constructing meaning. As Canney and Winograd (1979) suggest, learners' schemata for the act of reading affect how they read and make sense of texts. A teacher would want to demonstrate that reading is an active effort toward making meaning and not just recognizing words and saying them fluently.

As a beginning point, a teacher can encourage students to give the story an authorial reading. Every reader and every occasion for reading will offer a distinct rendering of the story, influenced largely by the reader's knowledge and personal connections with the story. But the fact is that an artist produced the story, having made conscious decisions about every detail of the product. When students are aware of a disciplined approach to reading literature, their point of entry into the text is both the authorial reading and the personal connection. Soto's story is likely to inspire connections, like Veronica's recall of her grandfather's story, and prompt discussion about the implications of the story. You can read much more about such discussions in chapter 8, with guidelines for prompting, extending, and monitoring discussions.

As a logical extension of the work with modeling the procedures for reading a narrative like "Like Mexicans," students will want to talk to their peers about their impressions of the story and their judgments about its thematic implications. The discussions should begin in small groups so that everyone has an opportunity to contribute. The teacher needs to frame an interpretive problem and not impose a long list of questions.

In grappling with the problem, the members of each group should find themselves drawing from the features of the text that they noticed (data) and the rules of signification (warrants) that allow them to draw conclusions from the details. For example, a teacher might ask, "How does the meeting with Carolyn's family at their home help to reassure him that he has not made a mistake in hoping to marry Carolyn?" or "Since the title of a story holds a privileged place, how is the title 'Like Mexicans' revealing about the whole story and its implications?" These problems look at the story as a whole, which is distinct from posing a list of questions that follow a taxonomic path to the understanding that the teacher has about the story. As students discuss the story as a whole, they inevitably come back to individual details to show how they have arrived at conclusions.

Extending the Practice

Of course, students do not identify and apply rules of notice and rules of signification with just one drawing and one story. As Ericsson (2017) and Gladwell (2010) report, in order for anyone to develop some level of expertise, the learner would have to practice, practice, practice. Chapter 3 suggests possible preparation for reading a satirical text like John Collier's "The Chaser." The story connects thematically to Gary Soto's "Like Mexicans."

As an option for an additional text to use to extend practice, "The Chaser" offers some advantages. It is a very short story, which would reduce the tedium of the teacher's demonstration or the students' taking turns to read aloud to each other as they reflect on what they notice, the events they anticipate, the questions they have in mind, and the meaning they construct. The story offers an additional view, perhaps an ironic or cynical one, to complicate a reader's conception of *romantic love*. If the old man in the story, and by extension the author, offers a critical view of the young man's breathless sense of ideal romantic love, how does the reader figure this out? What features of the text does the author expect an audience to notice and how do we know how to attach meaning to these elements of the text?

The point of further practice and the accompanying discussions is not to embrace the interpretation and evaluation that the teacher endorses, but to gain some facility with the procedures for reading a fiction narrative. If the learning suggested by the activities in this chapter is indeed *generative*, a group of adolescents would be able to read another story, report the meaning they have derived from it, and explain how they have arrived at their conclusions.

Summary of a Learning Sequence

Given that a teacher will reflect on a selected text and evaluate the kind of challenge they will present to learners, the teacher could design pre-reading activities that could activate prior knowledge and introduce critical questions about each text. This kind of task analysis that precedes the design of lessons requires the teacher to not only know a given text well but also know the learners well. This preparation can lead to the kind of lessons described in this chapter, lessons that emphasize modeling and practice with procedures for noticing features of the text and then constructing the meaning based on understandings about how humans behave, how language works, and how authors rely on conventions of storytelling. See Table 4.1 for a summary of a sequence of modeling and practice.

Table 4.1 Summary of Modeling and Practice

Step	Purpose	Impact
Model	The teacher *models* the procedures for noticing and interpreting.	The sequence moves from image to simple text to more complex text.
Practice	The teacher facilitates *practice* with the rules derived from reactions and discussion.	Practice can involve the teacher working with the whole class, but it should also include students working in pairs or small groups and ultimately on their own.
Extend	The class *extends experience* with the text through discussion of implications of the narrative.	Students will want to do more than catalog what they notice and will want to talk about the conclusions they reach and the assessments they make.

YOUR VIEW

The sequence of activities outlined above suggests the scaffolding of learning and attention to the connections across texts. You might question this sequence and the necessity for the designing learning experiences with a series of connected texts. You will likely find it helpful to discuss doubts and alternatives with your peers.

1. If the sequence described above in this chapter makes some sense to you, you might find yourself reflecting on other possibilities for illustrations to use or short stories to read. Talk to one or more colleagues about the potential for using other pictures and other short narratives to model procedures and to help learners to derive "rules" for reading a literary text.
2. Short story anthologies often seem to be a random collection of narratives, perhaps organized to illustrate and emphasize conventional story elements or to showcase the work of writers that editors have deemed important. How important is it that students are able to read and discuss narratives that connect thematically or conceptually and depict conflicts and problems that resonate with most adolescents?

Chapter 5

Modeling, Sharing, and Practicing

The previous chapter offers a sequence of activities designed to help students to identify rules of notice and signification. Learners need to move on from these preliminary forays to practice what they have learned with genuine pieces of literature. It should seem axiomatic that learners benefit tremendously from the teacher modeling procedures for reading complex texts, drawing from students' contributions in the process, and planning opportunities for students to practice the procedures. Teachers have a major role to play in getting their students to read for fun and for intellectual and emotional growth. Such growth ultimately requires mastery of skills and learned behaviors that are best taught through engineered experiences, and these require students to practice repeatedly as they read.

Such circumstances require that their literature teachers do far more than attempt to transmit thematic distillation, plot points, and character sketches, as if to do the reading for students. Instead, teachers create and engineer literary experiences for students who will, by their *active* engagement, progress from novice literary learners to more mature readers and enthusiasts of their storytelling culture. Although it is not popular to cite Ezra Pound (1934/1958) these days, when he did speak of literature, Pound wisely suggested many years ago, "culture starts when [readers] can DO the thing without strain" (22). In other words, learners need many experiences with reading literature and many opportunities to practice the procedures that mature readers rely on as they read complex texts.

What's an energetic and ethical teacher to do? One solution is free reading, imitating at school what students do at home: flipping dials until one sees something fun, familiar, and requiring relatively little of the mind. Some thoughtful, experienced teachers advocate letting students pick out any literary work (or nonfictional prose) they please and read just for the fun of it. No one, adult or child, would reject having fun with a preferred book, in contrast to slogging out a dirty sink or sticking with a seemingly boring book assigned by the teacher.

The problem, however, is that those advocating young readers learn what or how to read by relying on mere exposure, the tastes of friends, worst of all, the commercial selling strategies of book publishers for whom selling a good novel is no more relevant to their concern for the bottom line than promoting a celebrity cookbook, or a tell-all by a recently dismissed former U.S. Cabinet member. In this way, a whole generation may be shortchanged in learning a storytelling flexibility.

Many adults who are free-reading advocates have already learned how to get lost in a book (Nell, 1988) and already know the joys that printed verbal enchantment can bring. Although such adults can move on to other media after being fully grounded in techniques of story reading and analysis, they may be a little too quick to insist, as James Paul Gee (2007) has, that "once we see this multiplicity of literacy, we realize that when we think about reading and writing, we *must* think beyond print" (18; emphasis added). Why "must"? Certainly, adolescents now live in a digital world, but *must* we go "beyond print" *before* we've mastered the skills that good reading requires?

YOU HAVE TO SHOW THEM

Our arguments assume that teaching reading and teaching *how* to read literary texts—fiction and drama in print or in *live* performance—remain one of the primary tasks of English teachers. Kylene Beers (2003) wisely identifies that her goal is "to move dependent readers—whether that . . . sleepy one who sits in the back of the room, or the quiet one . . . in the middle, or the class clown who enjoys the front row—toward independence" (16). Dependent readers "depend on an outside-of-themselves source" to help them or even do the reading for them. Even very bright students need some guidance in learning how to make the most of their cultural knowledge and reading skills, and no amount of free reading by itself will guarantee a student's developing literary sophistication any more than a brilliant young soccer player will move into the upper athletic levels of competence without some skilled coaching.

The obvious question to explore then is HOW? This book offers to show how to teach verbal storytelling so that novice readers can ultimately engage in novels, stories, and plays without strain. When it comes to learning HOW to read much young adult fictions that are, after all, often rather formulaic in characterization or in relation to the elements of the plot, many scholars of teaching secondary students feel stuck on the twin difficulties of avoiding getting too complicated for beginning readers of challenging fiction, or so simplifying the task to the point where teaching is hardly worth the effort.

One answer comes again from Kylene Beers (2003), who reminds us that "summarizing a short story or a novel appears too overwhelming for many students, who either offer nothing or restate everything in the story" (145). This is not too surprising since, as she states explicitly, summary is something they cannot do easily (nor can many adults), yet that is exactly what teachers are often asking learners to do on the fly. Sometimes, to begin class, teachers ask about a story's theme, the particular emphasis that gives the tale what Rabinowitz (1987) calls its *coherence* or *unity*.

But as Beers suggests, when such a question comes *before* the discussion and not at the end of it, the too typical result is frustration and confusion. The best answer a student can give when the teacher asks for the "theme" of a story only partially understood is: "darned if I know!" While honest, and if not said in a spirit of mischief, such a response remains unsatisfactory.

Benjamin Bloom reminded his students often that if you want learners to do something, like read a complex work of literature, you have to show them how to do it. So, *modeling* is what good teachers do. For example, a responsible teacher who want to teach *process* can *show* students that in many mystery novels, for example, clues of the author's intentions are dropped in the first few pages and, for the experienced reader, only a few of those clues need to begin coalescing before allowing the reader to suspect some patterns.

Such clues might include an uncommunicative family member or partner, a time signature out of sync, odd objects found where they should not be or even missing, and so on. Finally, by the end of a satisfying mystery, especially one involving the major figure of a detective, critics like Hartman (1972) assume that this genre is in a "form in which appalling facts are made to fit a rationalistic moral pattern" (31).

Then, once facts and motivations are understood, the teacher may ask about labeling the theme, because by then, crucial information has been added to the mix and the novice reader's primary task is to try to put it all together. If the genre is an easily accessible classic (i.e., predictable) and not made to surprise completely, the detective story puzzles and solutions become "well-formed problems," where applying a given algorithm yields the *right* answer. In literary study, however, the most commonly used algorithm-like summary is called the genre, a type of story where plots and characters are known because they are historically familiar and their outcomes expected.

On the other hand, many literary works can best be thought of as ill-formed problems which do not yield particular and conclusive answers. In fiction, ill-formed problems mirror real-world conflicts where "facts" are conflicting or inconclusive, where characters may disagree for often unstated reasons about appropriate assumptions or theories, or where their values are in opposition. Detectives or scientists in novels may propose different solutions to the problem, each with particular strengths and weaknesses. In approaching an ill-formed problem, the thinker must attend to alternative points of view and create arguments justifying the proposed solution. A novelist responds to a well-structured problem with a "right answer," but, having set in motion an ill-formed problem, displays a character's claims and justifying arguments.

Good teachers try to persuade or encourage confused readers into separating generic fiction between the predicable and the surprising; hence, fiction whose themes and/or characters are predictable might appeal to novice readers. However, the greater the reading skills are developed in a novice, especially novices who prefer to be challenged, the sooner they become uninterested in further iterations of the predictable, and seek out fiction that, for them, surprises.

Once we have a sense of what to expect—the type of work we have completely read and are now ready to discuss—we can then consider whether or not our original set of expectations were ultimately fulfilled, or whether the author(s) gave us a work that may have seemed initially to be a given genre but was modified in some fashion. If so, *how* (and more importantly, *why*) was the tale modified? When Rabinowitz (1987) labels a piece of literature as "genre bound," one understands that asking students to label it *when finished* is merely an alternative means of analysis, a way of working out how to discuss an imaginative text that first appears to a novice reader as strange and puzzling. How does any English teacher begin with novice readers?

Teachers must remind themselves that the contemporary generation of movie enthusiasts is experienced in some ways, and even minor experts on "block-buster" summer fare, actually genre pieces such as *Wonder Woman*, *Batman*, *Spiderman*, and so on, for sure have already experienced in this domain insights into labeling types of films. The problem is not that they are unable to distinguish among a variety of genres on film or TV but, after all, one superhero usually performs unbelievable feats of strength and skill, representing law, justice, and moral rectitude.

The difficulty is getting a novice reader to discriminate the same with characters in the printed word. Instructing them to learn the patience and the willingness needed to do so is hard, for they must do things: to pull back from the specifics of character analysis and progressive movement far enough to see the readily understandable patterns of the genre, including what Phelan (1996) calls the *progression* of the narrative: "Progression refers to the way in which a narrative establishes its own logic of forward movement (. . . dynamic experience), and it refers to the way that movement carries with it invitations to different kinds of responses in the reader" (90).

Phelan's definition of "the progression" is important and worth pausing to understand how and why anyone reading a lengthy work needs to be familiar with the process of reading as a dynamic movement for both author or narrator and reader. Character trait lists—as examples of what could be called type-casting in Hollywood—are rarely useful while reading a good novel or story. Instead, Phelan argues that many characters, but not all, evolve or change as we experience them during the reading of a long work. So too do *we* evolve at the same time and change our opinions in short-term life experiences and in our emotions during the process of reading the work. In changing, we may rethink our opinions of characters or of people who think differently than we have or so do now, and/or so do our opinions of the author's values and his/her ideas.

MODELING FROM THE BEGINNING

Drawing from some concepts from Rabinowitz (1987), Phelan (1996), and Beers (2003), the following example illustrates some instructional practices with a story by John Henry Noyes Collier, a British writer of short fiction. Some of his tales can be very intense in an odd way to middle school and young high school readers similar to his story, "The Chaser," that became a program on the wonderfully weird TV program during 1950s and 1960s called *The Twilight Zone*. The story is often anthologized, and it can extend an inquiry into the concept of *romantic love*, perhaps introducing a cynical view to add to the more positive expressions discussed in chapter 4.

Our task as teachers will be to help novice readers (who will only have a printed text in front of them in the classroom) to learn how to identify the genre from early cues. Then by using their newly discovered knowledge of what to expect, they answer a couple of simple questions—to themselves and to each other before they explain their choices to the teacher.

Again, in following a read aloud/think aloud protocol, the teacher models for the novice reader to consider carefully what the author pushes us to look at. This push is supplied by the trio of the author—via what is called *focalizing*—by word choice, voice tone (imagined), visualization, and actual simulated bodily feelings (Caracciolo 104–5). When a teacher asks students what details they *notice*, they may focus first on the title, "The Chaser" and ponder its possible meanings—perhaps a pursuer or the more pleasant and softer second drink after someone consumes strong liquor, as in a shot followed by a beer "chaser." Could either or both of these meanings apply? Are there more possibilities.

Students might mention an unintroduced character, Alan Austen, being "nervous as a cat," climbing "dark and creaky stairs," and looking at "dirty buff-colored walls." How many mystery/horror films include a character climbing stairs and looking at a closed door with danger-ahead musical sound track, leaving us to wonder what's on the other side of it? Alan notices an old man in a rocking chair and a narrator tells us about the old man's voice being "very polite." The polite old man reminds Alan that "nothing I sell has effects [that are] ordinary." The old man's first example of his rather low key, yet proud boast is an "expensive life cleaner," an unusual, albeit euphemistically named, substance but clearly understood as poison, and Alan is "horrified."

The teacher may speculate why the polite old man uses a euphemism, and to wonder also why the polite old man mentions that to start? In effect, wondering out loud is what good teachers do to represent overtly what most experienced readers do (or should do) silently. Without direct mention, the teacher models this behavior in the same, sometimes, offhanded way that a coach informs a star soccer player to move just so in a particular context on the field.

In concentrating on the early passages of the story, a teacher might ask an authentic question, and the following exchange would ensue. This is a composite drawn from discussing the story dozens of times with high school students.

Ms. Victor: So, what do we know so far? Alan ascends a creaking stairway and enters an old man's dingy room. Does this story's progression so far give you the impression that something bad is going to happen?
Janey: The polite old man doesn't appear at all threatening to me.
April: He tells Alan that he realizes that he knows what the young man needs from him (student reals out loud): "It's only when one is in a position to oblige that one can afford to be so confidential."
Ms. Victor: So, so far, does the story remind you of horror stories you might know?
Cletus: I don't know. I don't think it is a horror story. There isn't anything really threatening. He is just going to an old guy's apartment.
Elena: If he is looking for a love potion, it won't be a frilly, romantic, happy-ending story either.
Ms. Victor: Anyone want to guess yet what we should expect?

The joint effort of the teacher and the students to speculate about the direction of the story sets up an environment of mutual discovery so long as the teacher maintains her own puzzling concerns (whether "real" or "enacted"). Not displaying answers here is at least as helpful as the more forced and typical question-and-answer routine that Nystrand (1997) has labeled "drill," where the teacher asks mostly questions with prespecified answers. Almost all veteran teachers have had a "discovery" or "ah-ha" experience in class with a text taught many times before, and they often come from a stale-mated question or an insight from a student who sees something novel or unexpected.

Such "discoveries" while spontaneous seem to be actually built-in to a lesson plan where the text has been a source of speculation and inquiry in previous iterations of class discussions. Conversely, mutual discoveries may also stem from something as mundane as the teacher's lack of preparation on that particular day. By not knowing all the answers, the teacher is, counter-intuitively, more effective, at least temporarily (cf. Showalter, 2003), as she enters with students into an area of doubt.

Ms. Victor: Returning to the story, we see that the polite old man answers Alan's questions about the "quality" or reliable effectiveness of his goods, and insists—maybe to Alan's initial satisfaction?—that the potion's effects (Ms. Victor reads out-loud): "are permanent . . . bountifully, insistently" (and Ms. Victor pauses and emphasizes): *"Everlastingly."*
Sylvia: Does that mean he'll give us details what the potion will do?
Cletus: Yeah, but Alan cries out, *"That* is love." The "that" isn't clear, is it?
Lily: Isn't love supposed to be "everlasting" anyway? "Til death do us part" and all that stuff?
Jaime: Why is that word "everlastingly" used—like emphasize? Right word for, after the stop?
Lily: The old man seems to agree—about that's love—and then tells Alan that even "if he slips up (since there are always sirens) . . . she will forgive you, in the end."
Jaime: Weird: Why does the polite old man repeat the last three words, repeated twice in a row?
Cletus: I don't know. I guess the polite old man tells Alan what he wants to hear.
Ms. Victor: That's curious (no further comment).
Janey: I am still bothered by the polite old man. What the potion will do is make the girl friend really clinging—like, *forever*. Maybe that sounds good to the guy right now, but he might find it annoying after a while.
Cletus: Then he would want like an anti-potion to get rid of her.

As the students continue to make their way through the story, either with the teacher's guidance or with a partner, they are likely to notice that Alan, now primed for the elixir of his dreams, asks the old man for the cost, and is told it's "not as dear . . . just a dollar," intimating to the alert reader that the word "just" seems emphasized but the old man offers no further explanation. In interrogating what appears to be a surprise to Alan, who wonders how such a valuable item would be so inexpensive, students are likely to notice that the polite old man expects Alan to return as a customer, and perhaps in a more desperate situation at a time in his life when he wants "more expensive things." The obvious cost-comparison issue seems to have been answered obliquely, and, again, the teacher models the "why" without offering a final answer.

Ms. Victor: One of the things we have to figure out is the old man assumes that Alan will want more expensive things later in life.
Sarah: It's not just Alan. When you're an adult, you work, make lots of money and want more things, right?
Ms. Victor: Some do; some don't. Let's look at the end more closely.

As the class looks again at the end of the story, they notice that as the characters part, the eager buyer expresses his gratitude while the seller reminds him again that he's more than likely to return "later in life, when they are better off." Students notice that the polite old man bids the young man farewell, not with the decisive "good bye," but *au revoir*, suggesting that they will inevitably meet again before long.

Janey: So, why does the polite old man use French when he says goodbye? What does au revoir mean anyway . . . in this context?
Sylvia: That's like goodbye, in French.
Jaime: So, why French? What's the difference? Why doesn't he just say goodbye?
Ms. Victor: Good question, Jaime. Some of you have taken French. Does *au revoir* mean exactly "goodbye"?
Sylvia: No. It's more like "until we meet again" or "see ya later."

So, what appears to be a satisfactory transaction that ends the story, and it allows us to reconsider what we have learned about it in contrast to any speculation on its genre we may have developed early on; we may wish now to reread, speculate, and reconsider it. Using the skills, Rabinowitz has referred to as "reading from memory" (1987, p. 92), the reader may now wish to comprehend the whole, finding its unity as she or he continues trying to comprehend the arc of the plot, based not on earlier recitation but on the much more immediate details jointly uncovered in the class exploration. In short fiction, the reader must be counseled that no point is resolved consensually, no analysis can be finally helpful before the whole story is completed, and then the genre is open for speculation and debate.

The story might appear rather simple and not require the kind of pre-reading activity suggested in chapter 3. But a teacher might share that the situation appears in one form or another often in literature, from *Doctor Faustus* to *Damn Yankees*. The teacher might recall Johannes Goethe's *Faust*, and the very familiar Faust theme: selling one's soul to the devil to gain supernatural powers, and thus enabling the buyer to get what she or he wants in the short run. In the long run, however, the bargain is often as costly as the sacrifice of one's soul. The teacher might ask, "Is the same thing likely to occur here? How would we know?"

At such a point, the teacher remains silent for a few minutes, and then tells the class to return to the details, via Rabinowitz's "Rules of Notice," in the short story. She might begin by asking: Why does the old man mention a potion as a "life cleaner," one costing five thousand times more, "never a penny less," than the love potion? What does the old man imply when he notes that sometimes lives need cleaning? John Collier assumes that, eventually, some reader may see the dawn light in Collier's refashioned tale that indeed depends on the reader's growing awareness of the "very polite old man's" charming voice to appear, thematically, like the serpent in the Garden of Eden in Milton's *Paradise Lost*: "With serpent Tongue/Organic, or impulse of vocal Air,/His fraudulent temptation thus began" (Bk IX, 530–31).

Now the likelihood of the average American middle school or high school student knowing of *Paradise Lost* or the Faust legend is relatively low, but, as suggested in earlier work (McCann and Knapp, 2019, pp. 13–14), the teacher's knowledge of broad and varied body of literature is important and, as part of educator's growing expertise, will often yield insights as unexpected as those illuminating Collier's little tale.

A bit of modeling and prompting allows the students to begin the process of connecting all the details in Collier's story to broad contours of the Faust theme as they begin to question the teacher (rather than vice versa) about whether the young man's actions in Collier's tale could relate to the Faust legend. Once learners make the relationships fit, the genre becomes clearer and then discussions of overall meaning shift from abstract literary terminology to more human details about what constitutes real love and the differences between intimate concerns about one's beloved versus obsessive demands and needs for absolute control.

If a set of related texts enriches students' inquiry into *romantic love*, this story offers a bitter element into otherwise idealistic and optimistic adolescent conceptions of romantic relationships. While this variation of the Faust legend is rather indirect—the polite old man may be tempting the young man as Satan did Eve by telling Alan just what he wants to hear—the "bargain" that Alan makes is as "everlasting" in his mortal life as selling one's soul to Satan is in one's spiritual life. Teacher explains the literary allusion but waits to see if students connect to "The Chaser," on their own.

CAN WE GET TECHNICAL IN TALKING ABOUT LITERATURE?

One of the more interesting pedagogical principles that Peter Rabinowitz (1987) recommends for middle school and high school readers actually has to do with instructing the teacher. The instructor who insists that students learn the vocabulary of literary study *before* they discuss a story or novel may actually turn off their charges well before they turn them on to storytelling. While the teacher may possess a ready-made mental container into which to insert new ideas and technical vocabulary, students usually do not.

To most high school students, "representations of literary consciousness," "narrative audience," "imagistic development," "discordant narrator," and "authorial audience" are mostly just abstractions requiring further reading experience in order for such terms to come alive as illuminators of elements in a literary text. Rabinowitz thinks that "technical literary language should be taught, but . . . taught on a need-to-know basis. Or, perhaps even better, technical literary language should be taught on a *desire* to know basis" (2014, p. 5).

So, how and when does the teacher share her greater technical knowledge with students, if ever? The big questions energizing literary vocabulary teaching always include how, when, and why. It is useful for the teacher to set or highlight a problem, one that might arise commonsensically as one reads to the end of a given story. To illustrate, let's look again at Gary Soto's often anthologized story, "Like Mexicans," which appears in the appendix. Before students reach the end of the story, they should look carefully at what the character-narrator, Gary, *sees* as much as what he *says*. This story could contribute to the ongoing inquiry into the concept of *romantic love*, if a teacher were concerned about the cohesiveness in a unit of study and were to connect this story to the texts discussed in chapter 4.

Chapter 4 shows a teacher and the students noticing some basic elements of the story. Later, they expand their attention to consider the genre-specific features, especially the author's choice of narrator. Analyzing a problem that students themselves have noticed or queried could help them understand better the narrator's (Gary's) summary at the end. It could also illustrate a student's "desire to know" a literary term or idea. However, since the reader of this book is likely a teacher or a teacher candidate, you should consider the technical concept of "representation of consciousness" in order to explore why an adolescent reader might desire to know what that means.

Consider a brief review of one technical concept. Suzanne Keen (2003) tells us this about much fiction:

> The representation of consciousness is one of the technical accomplishments that distinguish modern narratives, especially novels, from ancient precursors such as the Epic and the Saga. [T]his technical development arises in tandem with modern notions of the individual as a discrete self who possesses a rich interiority, an unconscious mind, memories, and partially recognized motivations . . . [and] suggests that the novel provides an especially flexible means of representing an aspect of experience (living inside a mind in the company of others who themselves possess minds) that modernity foregrounds. (59)

In other words, Keen observes here that the explaining of human awareness—self-consciousness of each person's own mentality—is one of the great fictional discoveries of the twentieth century.

Instead of thinking of other people as types or roles like soldiers, princes, bakers, and teachers, in modern fiction, people are now understood and judged by what they are thinking and believing as individuals, rather than as members of some group or caste or political organization, or for some role they may play in public. By giving us representations of what individuals actually think and feel, novels and shorter narratives allow us to look inward in the way that most nineteenth-century novelists consistently could not and did not do. Charles Dickens, for example, used to characterize most of his creations by transcribing their accents or odd turns of phrase—"by which I mean tur sai, Pip"—or describing what they wore, what they professed out loud, and what they did overtly in largely public ways.

While these ideas concerning the representation of consciousness are particularly important in understanding a long fictional form like the novel, they are also useful when trying to understand a much shorter fictional form like a story or remembrance told in retrospective narration, or even in a drawing. As explained below, new readers of fictional representations of mind may find shorter forms more readily understandable when some emotional conflicts appear familiar to their own experiences. Many authors of fiction, possessing the perspective-afforded maturity, try to represent their own memorialized debates as seemingly resolved when it's clear from their own prose choices that there may still be some problems in life that remain intractable.

In "Like Mexicans" (appendix), Gary Soto tries to explain his youthful thinking and emotional experiences over such conflicts that at first reading seemed to have been resolved: those internal conflicts between the person one has become emotionally as she or he is entering uncharted adulthood versus the family pressures to remain familiar and so fulfill what one's family and/or close friends have come to expect. Indeed, Soto's representation of his youthful self-consciousness makes clear that some conflicts are not and may never be settled.

His example of the painful emergence from a chrysalis to a developed butterfly begins with Soto's story about life in his early teens and growing up. At age twelve, he is already concerned about whom to marry, and his memories of that time are told with what is typically referred to as a first-person singular voice. Suzanne Keen (2003) reminds us that the term "first-person narrative," or self-narration, indicates those narratives "in which the character is also a narrator, where the narrator and characters coexist in the *story world*, and the narrator refers to himself or herself as 'I'" (37). Another major scholar, James Phelan (2018), calls such narrative voices as "character-narrators" (8).

One variety of the first-person narrator, the experiencing self, is also the protagonist or central character. Sometimes called fictional autobiographies, these narratives do not differ formally from actual autobiographies. First person narratives may be either *consonant* (i.e., the protagonist-self is close to the experiences) or *dissonant* (perceptions altered by time or distance). For our purposes here, consider that in a *bildungsroman* (a German literary phrase for a novel of a "young person growing up"), the narrator may also show a *modulation* from dissonant to consonant presentation of her/his experiences, suggesting the person's growing maturity.

One way students learn to enjoy authorial reading is to pay close attention to who the narrator is and whether or not the narrative voice is associated with a character closely tied to her or him. Is there a difference between Soto's narrator voice, the *I* and the values he seems to be reporting from his grandmother? The narrator tells us, imitating her voice, that "my grandmother gave me bad advice and good advice when I was in my early teens" concerning ultimately two life-changing decisions: become a barber "because they make good money and listened to the radio all day," and second, "marry a Mexican girl," but "no Okies." Her son "marry one, and they fight everyday about I don't know what and I don't know what."

Ms. Victor: Does his voice sound like a Mexican grandma? Do any of you know what one sounds like? How did you figure this out?
Sylvia: Yes she does because she kinda repeats herself, like "I don't know what."
Jaime: No, she doesn't because she speaks mostly English, with a couple of Spanish words thrown in.
Ms. Victor: We may not agree, but maybe we all noticed that her advice includes something neither she nor the narrator will tell us. She. only hints at some things (reads out loud): As Gary's grandmother "lectured [him] on the virtues of the Mexican girl," she mentioned how well the girl could cook, how she "acted like a woman, not a man," and would tell [him] about a third "when [he] got a little older" Here is what I am wondering: Why as an adult does the narrator now withhold information from us, the readers, about the third reason? Isn't he old enough now to hear, or to remember hearing?

Jerron: Maybe it's gonna be a surprise.
Janey: It's probably about sex—not a surprise, but a kind of secret.
Jerron: Yeah, but the narrator's just Gary grown-up, isn't he?
Janey: So what? We don't know very much about him so far. Maybe he's uncomfortable about sex.

With attention to rules of notice applied to these few details, the reader is set up to pose some of the same few questions that young Soto might think, if not ask out loud: the "good advice" we can perhaps guess, but what was the bad? So, the class is invited to interrogate further:

Ms. Victor: In her advice, the grandma warns against marrying an Okie. What's an Okie?
Jerron: It's like a white person, or someone who isn't Mexican.
Ms. Victor: I think it has a history that goes back to the Depression, when a lot of people moved from the interior of the country to California. So, what does the definition of an *Okie* have to do with the "third reason he should marry a Mexican girl [that] he'll be told when he's older"?

As readers ponder some basic navigational questions that the reporting character encounters, the teacher can only hope that student readers recall the information learned the previous day, and mentioned in Suzanne Keen's description (see before) of what is a first-person narrative? But typically, they may not. Then what's a poor teacher to do? Rather than worrying too much in the moment about correctly identifying the type of narrative voice we readers are hearing, our emphasis will be on *how* young Gary learns about the world in which he is growing up. The questions the teacher might consider asking could include these.

In this example, a class has moved together through a short story and highlighted what they noticed. But the *noticing* is only a beginning that leads to questioning and reflection. Students are likely to have their own questions, but a teacher might offer these questions for small group or whole class discussion: How many voices are we hearing in what we are told? Is there a distance and are there differences between Gary, the experiencing character who tells us how he thinks or feels what other characters say or do, vs. the reporter-Gary telling us with an objective sense about that time in his life? If so, how do we know and what does it matter, if it does? How does knowing those differences further our understanding of the tale?

The teacher and the class might press on together to construct meaning from the story and evaluate the merits of the implications. With his own question still unsettled, Gary mentions his grandmother's and mother's answers to his question as he states to his best friend privately: "No offense, Scott, I said with an orange slice in my mouth, but I would never marry an Okie," consulting his best friend, he asks, "Scott, a second-generation Okie," who reverses the insult: "No offense, Gary, but I would *never* marry a Mexican" (emphasis in the original). The narrator continues: "I looked at him: a fang of orange slice showed in his munching mouth. We walked in step, almost touching, with a sled of shadows dragging behind us. . . . I didn't think anything of it. He had his girl and I had mine. But our seventh-grade vision was the same: to marry, get jobs, buy cars and maybe a house if we had money left over."

Ms. Victor: What do you <u>notice</u>? Can you, the reader, see any differences between that "seventh grade vision"—that is, Gary as he thought in seventh grade—and the narrator reporting the specifics of his vision as an adult?

Edgar: Like a lot of guys, all they can think of is buying cars.

Jaime: So what? When I was in seventh grade, all I wanted was a motorcycle. I never got one.

Sylvia: You wanted a car. I wanted an expensive dress for my sister's wedding.

Ms. Victor: Any common denominator among all the things you wanted just a few years ago?

Jaime: What's a "common denominator?" You mean like math?

Ms. Victor: Sort of, but more like what do these visions have in common?

Edgar: When I could drive, I was grown up. Until then, I was still just a kid with dreams.

Sylvia: My sister getting married meant I had my own room and could sleep as late as I wanted.

Ms. Victor: Do you still want what you did in sixth or seventh grade? Could any reader tell yet, early on, when the characters are 12 or 13, who will be the most influential later, when Gary is, let's say, 20? Will it be Gary's grandmother? His mother? His friend Scott? Is there evidence to support one's hypothesis?

Jerron: Later in the story, he said when he "fell in love with this other girl," and shows both his grandmother and mother her picture. His grandmother thinks she looks Chinese. Then he said, "I was in love and there was no looking back."

Ms. Victor: To whom was he talking? His grandmother? Mother? The reader?

Sarah: He's not talking to anyone. He's like thinking out loud.

Jerron: It looks that way, but someone wrote this, so he's talking to the reader.

Ms. Victor: Gary told his mother who, he remembers, as always doing something with "slapping round steak," or "slapping hamburger into patties." He repeats this, so we said it is something we should notice. Why that image of her slapping meat? Has his mother's opinion changed?

Janey: No change. Gary then says that the "more I talked, the more concerned she became."

Lily: I do that too. I toss in bed at night worrying about my grades and friends. It says here what Gary says: "Later I began to worry. Was it all a mistake? Marry a Mexican girl, I heard my mother say in my mind."

Ms. Victor: So what became of his worrying? Did anyone else tell him who to marry?
Cletus: Gary did say, "I asked Scott, who was still my best friend, and he said, 'She's too good for you, so you better not.'"
Ms. Victor: So, Gary's problem is still unresolved. I wonder why?

Gary, the character-narrator appears to have been struck suddenly, so he tells us, with a solution, "like a baseball in the back." The issue is not so much ethnicity but social class: "my mother wanted me to marry someone of my own social class—a poor girl," and although "my fiancée, Carolyn, . . . didn't look poor, . . . I worried about it until Carolyn took me home to meet her parents." The rest of the tale is a discussion of that trip and one needs to ask if that trip resolves the problem given how we read about Gary's statement at the end? One typical way is by carefully listening to the voices, sounds, and images Gary employs to end the story. He tells us directly: "I felt happy, pleased by it all . . . her people were like Mexicans, only different." A teacher might press further into this area of doubt.

Ms. Victor: Is that it? Do you believe him? Does that line end questions about the story? Does the whole story fit together with this end? And I want to know how you figured things out.
Sarah: Yes and no. Since Gary repeated his "mother slapping meat image" before and that seemed important, I think he really was happy. Isn't that what he wants: to be happy and married?
Ms. Victor: Do the two go together for Gary? He seems to say so? Does he feel it, too?
Olivia: He says he's happy. If he says it, it must be true?
Jerron: Why? I sometimes think one thing but say something different. I don't know why.
Jaime: Ah, maybe his mom slapping meat is like what he can expect a Mexican woman like his grandma describes to be doing all the time. Maybe he thinks he can marry someone who is different. Maybe he wants someone different.
Ms. Victor: We talked about noticing images that are repeated. Are there any other mental pictures or images Gary repeats at the end? What do you notice about what he sees as he and Carolyn comment about what he's perceiving about her home?
Sarah: He tells us he sees like a bunch of junk (reads): "newspapers piled in corners, dusty cereal boxes and vinegar bottles in corners," and then a "kitten crawl up the window screen."
Cletus: Yeah, he tells us that, here: "the kitten opened its mouth of terror as she crawled higher, wanting in to paw the leftovers from our plates."

Janey: I don't get why Carolyn said he cat was "just showing off." When do cats "show off"?

Ms. Victor: (Reading from the story) "I looked in time to see it fall. It crawled up, and then fell again." While Gary feels uncomfortable about the cat's apparent hunger, Carolyn dismisses it, saying first it was "being silly."

Sylvia: Again, Carolyn says something weird: How can a cat be silly?

Ms. Victor: I wonder why Carolyn thinks so.

The story invites a lot of questions, including what it would be like to be in the position as Gary is in. Many adolescents have thought about Gary's tension in one form or another. In working through the text, a student or the teacher might note the obviously emphasized image of a kitten clinging to the screen on the door of the home: Why does the author want you, the reader, to pay attention to the fact that Gary notices the kittens? The image of the kittens on the screen appears "at a climactic moment," [their pictures] "repeat more than once," and "appear blatantly irrelevant" (Rabinowitz, 1997, pp. 54–65).

Ultimately, the issues center around what Keen (2003) terms a *discordant narrator*:

> Discordant narration makes a useful supplement to the terms "reliable" and "unreliable" for those cases where the narrator imparts information about events accurately but displays attributes that jar the reader and seem to clash with the views attributed to the implied author. (59)

As students discuss the contrasts between what Gary feels in the moment vs. what he sees upon reflection, as represented in the last paragraph, a teacher might revisit these questions: Does Gary feel happy? Or does he feel otherwise? How do you know and is there textual evidence in the story to point to, or are his feelings more implied than overtly articulated?

Finally, without knowing much about Soto's biography, students may be curious about his love at this point in his life for a member of "the other" group. In generalizing from the events of the story, a teacher might ask: "Does everyone who considers marriage approach the prospect with some ambiguity?"

In literary terms, we readers have moved from *rules of notice*—seeing detail—to putting several of them together so they collectively become *significant* in order for the reader to rethink the main character's motivations? Good writers usually don't spell out the meanings behind what readers are seeing, but in this case, getting married seems to have been a preoccupation of Gary's since seventh grade.

So, a class might begin by asking what IS marriage? What is *love* and *love alone*? Such significant questions and *noticed* details appear to *configure* into a kind of philosophy Gary has been considering for years. Does marriage have something to do with finding a life-companion who sees joining up with someone who was "like a Mexican"—his familiar family—or someone both alike and different? Does he see himself clawing like a cat to get into such a joint life, or does he prefer someone less anxious about belonging, one who can see the clawing cat as "silly" or "showing off," and not frightened or lonely? Someone who can pat his thigh and tell him it's going to be okay? Not every story or marriage ends with coherence and unity. As Ms. Victor said above, "Some do; some don't."

FROM SIMPLE TO COMPLEX

With the inclusion of the texts in chapters 4 and 5, the examples so far are some fairly simple texts, and it is reasonable to connect them as part of an ongoing *inquiry* into the concept of *romantic love*. Ultimately, teachers will want to move forward in two ways: moving from learning experiences that depend on the direction and modeling of the teacher and toward more independent effort. If learning has been "generative," then learners should have sufficient command of procedures to apply them more independently. If they can't, it is hard to say that they have actually learned.

The second movement is from simple to complex. As a teacher moves a class away from images from popular culture, constructed texts, and relatively simple stories, the teacher would probably want to see students practicing with the procedures they have learned as they encounter longer, more complex texts.

Such lengthy, complex texts can not be reprinted in detail here, but imagine a teacher and a group of students extending an inquiry into a concept like *romantic love* through their reading of texts like Jane Austen's *Pride and Prejudice* or Samira Ahmed's *Love, Hate and Other Filters*. Readers should not reduce either of these rich novels to an aphoristic statement about love. After all, the novels invite our thinking about perception, class, prejudices in many forms, gender, identity, and many other complicated issues.

At the same time, each novel depicts characters that have strong emotional responses to others, feelings that they identify as *love*. Certainly, sorting out infatuation from romance from friendship from acquaintance is part of adolescent experience, suggesting that a point of entry into each novel is the questioning of the central character's attraction to another character or characters.

In either case, a teacher can follow the same modeling practices discussed in this chapter. Closely examining the opening of each chapter and invoking the rules of *notice*, *signification*, and *configuration* can help students to anticipate the arc of the narrative, question the motivations and actions of the characters, and interrogate the author's implications.

While readers can anticipate that certain characters will be together as couples by the end of the novel, the path will digress and the reader can question the ruptures to a smooth arc and examine how they were influenced to anticipate some events and outcomes that never occur. With either novel, or other texts of equivalent length and complexity, students have opportunities for extended practice with the procedures they have learned with shorter texts. Since either novel is episodic, a teacher can isolate specific episodes for extended discussion and reflection.

The next chapter discusses more details about *rules of configuration* and offers ways that students can draw from their own experiences with a variety of narratives in many forms to define for themselves some typical ways in which narratives are configured. Again, the instructional pattern moves students from reliance on a teacher's modeling and guidance toward greater independence in applying procedures, from familiar images and relatively simple texts to longer and more complex texts.

YOUR VIEW

English language art teachers are typically experienced and skilled in reading works of literature closely and critically. This means that the teacher commands some advanced intellectual moves. For us, an instructional key is for the teacher to make those moves *overt*. Talk to some of your colleagues about what you judge to be essential procedures for reading complex works of literature.

1. To what extent are there "rules" for reading literature? How much merit is there in helping students to *discover* such rules as "rules of notice," "rules of signification," and "rules of configuration"?
2. If you find the modeling procedures and the "rules" that we suggest are lacking in some way, where do they fall short, and what are the alternatives?
3. If you are going to *teach* students *how* to read literature, what can you do that moves well beyond assigning texts to read and then quizzing students about their reading?

Chapter 6

Seeing Patterns and Structures and Making Complex Inferences

This chapter offers the kind of inquiry- and discussion-based activities that can help students to become aware of common patterns of action for narratives. Some authors defy conventional patterns in innovative ways; yet, for adolescents studying literature, a recognition of typical configurations supports basic comprehension and recall and invites reflection on why the author organized the pattern of the action in a particular way. This chapter provides sample activities to help students to construct concepts about configurations of narratives and to encourage practice with the concepts.

It is possible to find oneself working with students who have had limited experience with reading literature of any kind or with viewing films. But even if students' experience with literature has only been through hearing older relatives or community members tell stories, they have likely built a body of knowledge about various kinds of narratives. Readers use this knowledge to help them to anticipate the course of action in a story or drama and to construct meaning about the texts by thinking about how the sequence of events (e.g., a rough start and series of obstacles for a character, leading to resolutions and a happy ending) has made them *feel*. Also, if the anticipated sequence of events takes an unexpected direction, the reader can speculate about the implications in this *rupture* to a conventional sequence (e.g., a young man and young woman long to be together, find a way, but then kill themselves).

As discussed in the previous chapters, it is useful for a teacher to build on students' knowledge of story structures to define some rules—in this instance, *rules of configuration*. There is clearly a futility in lecturing students about some conventional ways for configuring narratives or in assigning students to read descriptions of such structures. In the spirit of inquiry, a teacher can engage students in structuring stories themselves and reflecting on the decisions they have made to configure the narratives. The object of the group inquiry is that the students would describe how stories are often structured and how the opening episode of the narrative often reveals the direction of the narrative as a whole.

One value in having this awareness is that students can anticipate the pattern of the action, which helps them to process the events of the story (Mandler and Johnson, 1977). When the story takes a turn that runs counter to the anticipated direction, the reader can reflect on the author's purpose in disrupting the usual course of events. Either way—the story goes in the anticipated direction or the story breaks with convention—the reader's awareness of what is going on, perhaps tying the structure to a tradition, helps the reader to interrogate the author's expectations, draw some conclusions, and critique the implications.

This chapter offers two sample activities ("Build Your Own Movie Treatment" and "Ezzat's Roman Connection") to help learners to become aware of what they already know about rules of configuration and then transfer this knowledge to their work with literary texts, both brief and extended. The instructional sequence follows in this three-step process: (1) Students engage in an inquiry-based, small group activity to generalize about the ways that stories are typically structured. This exploration should lead to students describing how the opening elements of a story typically define the direction of the narrative and suggest the general tone of the story and some thematic implications. (2) The teacher helps students to compile their list of rules, which can serve as warrants as students discuss the meaning they construct from a narrative. (3) Students practice with the rules as they work with a story that is likely new to them. This work includes discussion of the direction of the narrative beyond what the author has provided and evaluation of the thematic implications of the story.

The first activity draws on students' familiarity with narratives in popular culture, especially films, television programs, and popular fiction. Here is the general outline for the teacher:

- *Set goals*: Before beginning small group work and large group discussions, the teacher explicitly alerts students that their problem-solving and discussions will allow them to generalize about the ways that stories are typically structured. The rules that students identify will serve them as warrants as they explain how they have made complex inferences about a story. The awareness of common story structures will help students to follow the course of a narrative and interrogate why authors have organized narratives the way they have. The students should also be able to say generally what an author expects readers to recognize about the structure of the story and how they are likely to feel about the sequence.

- *Introduce the Problem*: The teacher distributes the "Build Your Own Movie Treatment" (below) and reads aloud the Basic Premise of the proposed movie.
- *Initiate Small Group Work*: The teacher directs students into prearranged groups and assigns a particular television channel to each group. Chapter 4 notes some basics for organizing small groups. The teacher reads aloud the directions for the small group work and sets a particular target outcome for the discussion (e.g., a completed narrative summary) and a specific time limit. A tight time limit at first can keep students focused, and then a teacher can extend the time as needed. Realistically, the whole sequence is at least a two-day process.
- *Monitor and Support Group Work*: There is a need to supervise the small group discussion, and you can find useful the suggestions from Forde (2019) and Bouque and Forde (2019) for assessing group work. This does not mean following each group with a clipboard and assigning points for contributing something to the group. Instead, the monitoring involves moving around the room and judging the level of engagement, the functionality of the group, the need for support, and the inclusion of all group members.
- *Facilitate Group Reports*: This probably will occur on the second day of the sequence. In a way, the fun begins when each group shares its movie treatment. In some instances, the narratives will be parodies of movies characteristic of specific channels, and some will be odd twists on the conventional storytelling. With the teachers' patience and help, the students can describe what guided their decisions in extending the story. The interchanges, then, should allow the class to generalize about the way stories are typically structured, how the pattern of the action makes them feel, and how the organization of events carries some thematic implications. As the teacher lists statements that sound like rules, the students can affirm that these are an accurate representation of the students' conclusions. Encourage students to record the rules that the class has constructed.

BUILD YOUR OWN MOVIE TREATMENT

The Basic Premise

After completing culinary school, Anna Damma began working with a baker named Matthew Levin. Matthew was a bit older than Anna and owned an urban bakery called Pan au Levin that featured naturally leavened breads made from "heritage" grains. Although the hours were long and her work days started very early, Anna loved her experience at the bakery and admired Matthew very much. After three years at the bakery, Anna and Matthew developed both a close working relationship and a valued friendship. Then Anna began to notice some changes in Matthew as the bakery became more popular and the demands to produce greater amounts of bread quickly became more intense. Anna was alarmed to discover that Matthew had begun to introduce "rapid rise" yeast to the bread doughs and began to purchase greater quantities of bleached all-purpose white flour instead of the more expensive heritage varieties that made the bread at Pan au Levin distinct. When Anna expressed her displeasure, Matthew dismissed her concern and suggested that she was too inexperienced to understand the business aspects of his enterprise. The disagreement developed into a major blowup, with Anna throwing down her apron and stalking out of the bakery, swearing never to return.

But what was Anna, who loved baking and had experience in only one shop, to do? Although Anna's parents had retired and moved to New Zealand, her aunt Gloria remained in Anna's hometown of Turkey Bridge, Virginia, near the Little Kanawha River. Anna decided to return to Turkey Bridge to reorient herself and find a new direction. When she arrived late one afternoon in Turkey Bridge with her few meager belongings, many things looked different from her childhood, and she found herself asking directions to a young man who was loading cement bags into the back of a pickup truck. The panel on the side of his truck read, "Baxter's Harvest: Produce and Handywork." "I am sorry," Anna said, "but things look so different." Pointing to an abandoned store, Anna asked, "Wasn't this the Custis Bakery?" "It was," the young man replied, "but Mrs. Custis grew too old to run the place, and some storm damage made it not worthwhile to try to repair. Anyway, folks buy all of their baked goods at the Walmart now. Who really needs a fancy bakery? Bread is bread."

Where Do We Go from Here?

Complete the movie treatment in a way that you judge to be consistent with the kind of movies that one of the following channels would support and program. Your team will develop a treatment for one assigned channel. To complete this project with your team, do the following: (1) Drawing from your knowledge of the way that narratives are structured, complete the story in a way that logically connects to the beginning and that is consistent with the types of stories that the channel would typically show. (2) If necessary, alter the beginning of the narrative (without radical changes) to prepare an audience for the direction it must take in the target context. (3) Considering how the narrative develops, characterize the prevailing *tone* of the story and describe the themes or problems that it suggests. How does the *structure* of the story itself convey a vision of the human condition or attitude toward life?

The Harmony Channel: Viewers of this channel like twists and turns in the narrative but want their expectations for a happy ending to be satisfied, usually through two persons working out problems to achieve a hopeful and harmonious situation for themselves and the community.

Real-Life Drama: Films produced by this channel depict the grim realities of life, showing situations that begin in a hopeful way but decline into a series of complications that, while not horrific or catastrophic, leave the viewer feeling sad and perhaps a little reflective.

Today's Detective: The name of the channel tells it all. Movies on this channel introduce a crime and invite the viewer to join with a central character in trying to detect the culprit.

Satire Central: The humor in the programs on this channel is typically dark, achieving both a humorous effect and bitter impression by disrupting the usual conventions of common genres.

Food TV: Generally, this channel offers "reality" shows and documentaries, but it has expanded into films that depict some aspect of food or the food industry, usually representing the difficult aspects of careers in the food industry or celebrating the work of a person or team of persons in the food industry.

The Adventure Channel: This channel features the adventures of a central character traveling through a perilous world to achieve an objective that will benefit many people.

Dark Night Channel: This channel specializes in gothic and horror tales. The experience with each of their movies is that the viewer has a constant sense of foreboding, as if something bad could happen to a central character at any moment, even if the character never experiences any physical harm.

What to Expect

Experience tells us that students have fun working with this activity. These features contribute to the enjoyment: (1) students draw from what they already know so that they feel confident in contributing, (2) students engage in everyday sort of problem-solving, as if they are simply watching a film with a friend and predicting where it will go, and (3) students are interacting with peers, which makes them feel connected, both to the members of their small group and to the class as a whole.

Every class will be different and require different kinds of support and perhaps a significant adaptation of the directions. But it has been our experience that students respond well to this activity and the outcome is that they increase their awareness of how stories are commonly structured, helping them to tackle a variety of narratives and talk about the sense they make of them. You can find below a brief example of a group's report.

Cam: We had the, whadya call it, the Harmony Channel. This is the kind of thing my aunt and my grandma watch all the time. It is always on when you go to their house.

Ms. Parker: So, what is your group's treatment?

Marie: You want me to read it?

Ms. Parker: Yeah, that would be nice.

Marie: At first, the young man, whose name is Travis, seems kind of rude and dismissive to Anna. She forgets him for the moment and drives off to her aunt's house. Her Aunt Sally brings her up to date on the changes around town, including her reliance on a guy named Travis to do some odd jobs around her house. Anna shares with Aunt Sally that it is a shame that the one bakery in the town is closed and appears to be beyond repair. But Aunt Sally says that the brick oven in the bakery was never harmed, it would be cheap to buy, and a handy guy like Travis could probably do the needed repairs. At first, Anna dismisses the possibility, but the next day she visits the old bakery, enters through a broken door, and sees that the shop with its brick oven has great potential. Noticing the open door, Travis goes in, startles Anna and then warns her that it is dangerous to stay in the dilapidated building. She recalls how she came to the bakery when she was a young girl and describes how she thinks the place still has a lot of potential. Travis is at first skeptical, but Anna persuades him that the bakery can be reconstructed and the attempt is a worthy cause. Anna's aunt lends her the money for the building. Together, Anna and Travis work very hard to make over the shop, until the exciting day when Anna fires up the brick oven again. But Matthew Levin, feeling bad about the falling out with Anna, has tracked her down in an attempt to get her to return to the city and his bakery. Travis fears that this slick young man from the city will convince Anna to return with him, but Anna rejects him and embarks on her new venture of Anna and Sally's Heritage Bakery. On the day it opens, Travis and Anna embrace and look forward to a promising future.

Ms. Parker: Somehow this movie sounds familiar. Can you tell me how your group figured out how to finish the narrative?

Silas: Well, like you know, these movies introduce two young people. One person is trying to sort of start her life over. At first, she doesn't like the guy, but then she finds something to like about him. And she is trying to start her career again. So the story has to show how she can be successful at what she likes to do, and then the two people fall in love. You could make the same movie but set it in December in a town that looks like the North Pole. That would be the Christmas version.

Ms. Parker: So, this sounds like a romantic comedy. As a rule, then, when a story starts out with two young people who meet but can't be together, they will probably be romantically involved, if not married, by the end of the story. If it doesn't work out that way, perhaps the author is confused or is implying some more negative view of life or relationships.

As these reports continue and the teacher prompts students to explain how they completed the treatment, the class constructs a set of rules that generalize how narratives are constructed. These are not rules that define how a story should proceed from the features of the text at the beginning of the story, but the expectations for the progress of the narrative as it is likely to take shape for an intended audience; for example, the viewers of a crime drama or the viewers looking for horror and gothic, and so on. Here are some rules of configuration that a class might define:

Rule of Attraction: Two young people are attracted to each other and someone or some force keeps them apart, yet they manage to overcome the obstacle(s) to be together in the end.
Rule of Suspicion: After a crime is discovered, suspicions fall on one or several possible perpetrators until an insightful person refuses to be misled and reconstructs the crime in order to identify the criminal.
Rule of Perpetual Tension: A pleasant and naïve character enters into a setting and situation in which the character can come to harm at any moment, yet the character narrowly survives several serious threats.
Rule of Downfall: A character experiences some good fortune but makes bad decisions that lead to a harmful or catastrophic outcome.
Rule of Journey and Return: A central character completes an arduous journey in order to battle a daunting enemy and bring some benefit to a community.
Rule of Success: A humble character experiences a series of problems, failures, and accomplishments in order to achieve some stature in a given field of endeavor.

These rules are not exhaustive and are different from the rules that Rabinowitz (1987) and Rabinowitz and Smith (1998) describe. Rules of configuration will be specific to a genre and will derive from an awareness of an audience for which an author intended a narrative. The learning impact comes from a class of students discovering for themselves that there are such rules, whether or not they recall the labels or the precise definitions.

Rabinowitz notes the usefulness of this third category of rules:

Third, by applying rules of configuration, readers can—during the act of reading—assemble the details and their significances generated by the first two sets of rules into some more or less familiar patterns, thus allowing them to make predictions about what is to come. (Rabinowitz and Smith, 1998, p. 56)

In contrast to more generalized encouragement for students to make predictions as they read, students need to be aware of patterns of narratives in order to be in a better position to predict and to question why the author relied on a conventional configuration or ruptured the anticipated pattern.

Practice with Rules

Teachers will recognize the familiar sequence of instruction proposed here: first, the class engages together in constructing an understanding of concepts; then they practice together in teams or pairs; in the end, each student functions somewhat independently to repeat the practice with new material. The focus here is on the small group practice. Instead of using a short story, a portion of a friend's memoir serves.

The narrative invites an empathic response that helps students to project how the narrative continues. Students have examined this narrative in class. Not only were the students readily able to project the course of the narrative and explain how they arrived at their conclusions, but they also were eager to know what actually happened in the end. The poet, playwright, and fiction writer Ezzat Goushegir generously agreed to share her story for instructional purposes. Below you will find a fragment of the story, titled "Ezzat's Roman Connection."

The instructional sequence follows in three steps: the teacher telling the fragment of the story, small groups discussing to project and explain an ending, and then the large group sharing and evaluating the projections. Near the end of a class, a teacher tells Ezzat's story, without providing the ending. The teacher might say that she regrets that she has run out of time to tell the ending, but encourages students to think about how the story would likely end. At the beginning of the next class meeting, the teacher organizes the class into groups, keeping in mind some grouping principles discussed in chapters 3 and 4.

In case anyone had been absent, the teacher repeats the story and asks the students in each group to provide an ending and to offer their rationale for why the story would end the way they predicted. The story follows here, and then a bit of the large group discussion in which participants offer their endings and then explain the basis for their prediction.

EZZAT'S ROMAN CONNECTION

During the oppressive and murderous reign of the second Shah of Iran, political dissidents and progressive artists found it both dangerous and suffocating to work under the control of the regime. Nevertheless, playwright and fiction writer Ezzat Goushegir and a small group of friends ran an underground newspaper that promoted liberal democratic ideas. If caught, those who worked on the newspaper could be imprisoned, tortured, and even executed. The newspaper operated in the shadows and the writers and editors continued their work without detection for a few years. But Ezzat knew that she needed to work in a more politically liberal environment if she were to have a chance to develop artistically and to expand her political thought. At the time, Ezzat had a five-year-old son. She confirmed with her husband that she could no longer develop as a writer under the current oppressive conditions and it was time for her to live, for a few months at least, with friends in Italy, where she could write creatively and express her political opposition without fear of reprisal from the Shah's regime. Ezzat managed to secure visas for herself and her son to be able to travel to Italy, and she confirmed with Iranian expatriates in Italy that she could stay with them in Perugia for six months to a year.

Ezzat hastened to put her affairs in order and pack essentials for a trip that might never include a return to Iran. As she and her son were waiting in the boarding area of the airport, she looked around repeatedly, expecting to see police moving toward her at any moment. Even when they had begun their flight, Ezzat could imagine government operatives or assassins waiting to abduct her upon her arrival in Italy. But mother and son debarked without any such incident and made their way to a bus that would take them to Perugia, where they could join Ezzat's friends.

After a month in Perugia, Ezzat learned that matters worsened in Iran. When thousands of protestors rallied in opposition of the Shah, he had the military under his command shoot them down, killing hundreds, including women and children. Provoked by this tragic event, Ezzat and some of her dissident friends in Italy decided to meet in Rome to participate in a hunger strike. She and her son soon boarded a bus and made their way to Rome.

Upon arriving in Rome and knowing no Italian, Ezzat could not read the signs nor ask anyone for directions. As she stood, confused, with one hand holding her son's hand and the other with a piece of paper with the name and address of a contact in Rome, a woman approached her and asked something in Italian.

The woman reached for the slip of paper and said, "Ah, si." She then gestured for Ezzat to take her belongings and her son and follow her. They walked to a ticket window, where the woman bought three bus tickets. She then pointed to a waiting bus. They boarded and the Italian woman gestured to two open seats, as if to welcome the newcomers. The bus lurched forward. No one spoke.

The bus ride continued for perhaps 20 minutes, but it seemed to Ezzat to be much longer. The bus was warm and crowded with other passengers. Ezzat worried about putting her fate and the fate of her son in the hands of this stranger. Then the bus pulled into a covered terminal. The Italian woman grabbed Ezzat's bag, headed toward the open door, and gestured for Ezzat and her son to follow. She walked briskly up a street. It was late afternoon, turning to early evening. Fatigued by the journey, Ezzat and her son struggled to keep up. They followed the woman through a maze of streets; then they passed down what seemed to be an alley. The Italian woman stopped in front of a two-story building. She looked up at the building and down at the slip of paper, then back at the building. She nodded affirmatively at Ezzat and gestured toward a door. The woman handed the slip of paper back to Ezzat, turned abruptly, and walked down the narrow lane.

Students' predictions about the outcome of the story can be influenced by whether the teacher tells the story as an anecdote relayed from a friend, or has the students read the story independently. How someone might tell the story can in itself convey expectations, revealed through inflection, gesture, and emphasis. The following example, drawn from a composite of discussions, illustrates a group of learners practicing with an awareness of narrative configurations.

Everett: You didn't say that your friend is alive, but we guessed that she must be alive if she was able to tell you the story. So she survived. That made us guess that she was at the right address and she was able to connect with the people where she was supposed to meet.

Beth: We said about the same thing. Only we thought that maybe the woman was sent by the friends to meet your friend at the bus station so that she would know where to go. She was scared and all but her friends were looking out for her.

Theo: We had something different. Yeah, she is alive, but we thought that some people sent by the Shah were waiting for her and they arrested and tortured her. The way the story is told, with the woman all nervous about people possibly following her and some mysterious Italian woman leading her, made us think that something bad was going to happen.

Ms. Parker: Tell me about some of the things you noticed that made you think something bad was going to happen.

Ruby: I am in Theo's group. We noticed, wait, here, "Ezzat could imagine government operatives or assassins waiting to abduct her upon her arrival in Italy." So she was all nervous about someone capturing her. That puts the idea in your head that something bad is going to happen.

Theo: It also says, "Ezzat worried about putting her fate and the fate of her son in the hands of this stranger." So you think that something bad could happen at any minute. She is in a strange place. She is following this stranger. She doesn't know where she is going. All that makes you think that something bad is going to happen.

Maria: It doesn't have to be like government agents. The woman might have been setting her up to be robbed.

Beth: But why then did the woman pay for the bus tickets and everything? We thought it was like a Good Samaritan story. Some special person just feels sorry for the woman and her son so she helps them find their way. So what really happened?

Ms. Parker: Let's hear some other conjectures.

Arjun: That could happen, like Beth says. I know that when my family arrived in London, we understood the language and all, but we didn't know our way around. A bunch of people asked us if we needed help and showed us how to get to my uncle's house. Sometimes when you're lost, people help you out.

Fortunately, with the help of a benevolent stranger in Rome, Ezzat and her son found their way to the correct address, where Ezzat's friends welcomed her and her son as they had planned. But the point of the discussion is not to guess the accurate outcome, but to draw from a familiarity with how stories are told and to point to the related features of the text that they noticed to be able to complete the narrative and reflect on its implications (e.g., diabolical plot or act of a Good Samaritan).

Further Practice with a Short Story

Although Ezzat's story is part of a developing memoir and is not fiction, it has much in common with some short stories and films. At the end of the episode, when someone opened the door in a town on the outskirts of Rome, that person was Ezzat's friend, who welcomed her and her son warmly. For the sake of discussion with students about the features of a narrative that might suggest the direction of the story, a teacher would leave off the ending of Ezzat's story. A teacher could readily find short stories that invite readers to imagine the outcome or the next episode. The following story, "Of Arms and the Wall," typically engages students in putting into practice rules of notice, signification, and configuration.

As suggested in chapter 4, the teacher could follow a read aloud/think aloud protocol to model at the beginning of the story how a mature reader would notice features of the text, reflect on the significance of those features, and anticipate the direction of the story. A good practice is to read the title and the first three paragraphs together with students and then turn the remainder of the reading over to the learners to complete on their own.

OF ARMS AND THE WALL (HOLLIS MAY)

A group of four teens gathered at the back of the Tastee Freeze at 87th and Aberdeen. Two of the boys looked into a canvas sack, while the boy holding the sack looked over their heads, as if scanning the landscape for something. The sack sagged, suggesting that it held heavy contents. One boy crossed his arms in front of him, perhaps supervising the proceedings.

Three younger teens viewed the scene from across the street. They sat on a low concrete barrier that defined the perimeter of the parking lot for the O'Neill Funeral Home. The teens in the area referred to the concrete structure as "The Wall." This name referred both to a location—as in "I'll meet you later at The Wall"—and to a group of guys who hung out there—as in "He's a member of The Wall."

The older brother of one of the boys sitting on the wall, along with three of his friends, awaited the result of the inspection of the canvas sack. "That's Blue Jesus," he said, tipping his head in the direction of the boys across the street, referring to the cross-armed observer, a dark-skinned Puerto Rican with blue eyes. "He's brought some heavy artillery."

One of the younger boys stood up. Melted custard from the cone he held dripped across the back of his hand. The other two boys looked at each other. "Where are you going?" demanded the older boy. "My mom wanted me home by 2:00." "You ain't goin' nowhere," the older boy insisted.

The two boys who had peered into the canvas sack crossed the street. In a hushed, conspiratorial tone, one boy reported, "Three handguns and a sawed-off shotgun." Blue Jesus and his companion walked away, moving down the alley, not the street. "He knows we are having trouble with those punks from Brainard, so he offered some firepower. That's what he said—'You guys need some heavy artillery?'"

The brother of one of the younger boys addressed the three young friends. "Those punks from Brainard are going to come by. You guys ain't goin' anywhere. If you are going to be part of The Wall and hang out here, you've got to defend The Wall."

"We didn't have any trouble with the Brainard guys. What would we be fighting about?"

"It don't matter. Those guys are against The Wall. If you think you are going to hang out here, you've got to defend The Wall."

"But it's getting serious. I don't want anything to do with guns. We never used guns."

Two cars cruised by slowly, eastbound on 87th Street. A voice boomed from the lead car: "The Wall sucks!" The opening salvo for a fight. "Come back here, you fags," someone shouted in return.

The younger boys stood up from The Wall.

"You punks ain't goin' nowhere."

They could all see the two cars making u-turns at Carpenter Street, headed back toward The Wall.

Students can readily point to features of the text that they judge the author wanted them to notice: for example, the title, the setting, the central characters, the threat of violence, the characters' reactions to danger, and the unfinished nature of the narrative that invites predictions. Students typically see a contrast between a child holding a melting ice cream cone while other young people are planning acts of violence.

A simple recitation of some details of the story is insufficient; instead, students will refer to them as they discuss implications of the story. A few interpretive questions can drive discussion: Given what the author probably planned for you to notice about the story, including its incomplete ending, how do you think the action is likely to play out? Considering what is likely to happen, what conclusions do you draw about the story as a whole? Do you judge that the author is using the story to comment on the behavior of adolescents alone, the behavior of adolescents in a particular circumstance, or suggesting some larger conclusions about human beings in general? What do you think the author is implying, and how were you able to arrive at your conclusions?

The act of reading is dynamic, with readers shifting predictions and conclusions as they move through a text and perhaps as they backtrack to reread certain sections. Rabinowitz comments on the use of our awareness of rules of configuration and the author's exploitation of the reader's knowledge:

> A reader applies previously learned rules of configuration while moving through the text. These rules are basically predictive—at least, on the level of discourse, although not necessarily on the level of story (that is, they permit us to make guesses about what will happen in the later parts of the text, whether the events described are chronologically before or after those we have already read about). They are therefore always probabilistic. To put it another way, in a given literary context, when certain elements appear, rules of configuration activate certain expectations. Once activated, however, these expectations can be exploited in a number of different ways. (p. 111)

In the brief narrative from Hollis May, the recognition of a pattern, with knowledge drawn from other reading or from life experience, allows the reader to predict the likely outcome of the story, which *involves* the reader in the narrative. Being able to say what *really* happened at the end is irrelevant, since the fun in the reading and the significance of the implications depend on the reader being able to say, with all probability, what would *likely* happen in such a situation.

Building on Practice

This chapter offers a fragment of a memoir and reproduced a very brief short story. Teachers will want to engage students in longer and more complex stories, both as practice and for the experience of literature as inquiry and exploration. The study of some commonly taught short stories will allow students to apply their knowledge of rules of configuration to support their reading, and will prompt their reflection on meaning and effect. Here are a few possibilities: Poe's "A Cask of Amontillado," Guy de Maupassant's "The Necklace," Leonard Ross's "The Path Through the Cemetery," Richard Connell's "The Most Dangerous Game," H. H. Munro's "The Interlopers," Hernando Tellez's "Lather and Nothing Else," Mona Gardner's "The Dinner Party," Chinua Achebe's "Dead Men's Path," Naguib Mahfouz's "The Answer Is No," and Liam Flaherty's "The Sniper." These tales are commonly anthologized or readily available online. Many printed and online collections offer a wealth of possibilities for short stories to enjoy and discuss.

In high school, teachers commonly assign students to read book-length works of literature, usually piecing out assignments, chapter by chapter or chunk by chunk. While short texts offer opportunities for practice with recognizing how narratives are configured and with drawing inferences about the significance of patterns of development, students should have other opportunities to sustain reading and recognize, anticipate, and question patterns in narratives, including drama, with longer texts that allow for shifts in the pattern of development or digressions from the conventional structure.

As emphasized in chapter 4, with long, complex works, it is helpful for the learners to attend closely to the opening of the work. As students discuss their projections for the likely continuation of the narrative, based on their awareness of rules of configuration, they can process and recall a plot and reflect on the implications of the configuration in itself, which provides a gateway into analysis of other aspects of the narrative. For mature readers, knowing that Fielding organized the episodes of *Tom Jones* in a configuration that can be seen as a set of concentric circles allows them to appreciate a larger, cohesive product and not a rambling and random series of actions. The series of meetings between the *Pequod* and nine other ships in *Moby Dick* can serve to bind the whole narrative together and reveal information and insights for Ahab and Ishmael. Similarly, high school students can discover and sometimes predict the configuration of Hinton's *The Outsiders* or Myers' *Monster*.

As Rabinowitz (1987) points out, "Calling a play *The Tragedy of Hamlet* is not that much more subtle a way of warning us about how it is going to end" (p. 114). When Jane Austen begins a novel by noting, "It is a truth universally acknowledged, that a single man in possession of a good fortune, must be in want of a wife," the reader can readily anticipate the direction of the narrative, especially if the reader has read any other Austen novel.

If students join their teacher in closely examining the opening of works like *Macbeth*, *Romeo and Juliet*, and *Pride and Prejudice*, they can manage their way through texts that might otherwise present frustrating challenges.

The recognition of rules of configuration does not mean reducing narratives to simple formulas. Rabinowitz offers this distinction:

> Rules of configuration are prescriptive only in the following way: they map out the expectations that are likely to be activated by a text, and they suggest that if too many of these activated expectations are ignored, readers may find the results dull or chaotic. (p. 113)

YOUR VIEW

In your own experience as a student and in some of your initial attempts to teach literature, you have probably seen others who have sponsored the use of graphic organizers or structured note-taking frames to help readers to represent a narrative as a cohesive whole, with an emphasis on recalling the plot. This chapter moves beyond recall as a goal, although being able to summarize is an essential skill, and have suggested that a recognition of how a narrative is configured can help the reader to construct meaning and evaluate the implications. Any teacher is likely to benefit from conferring with colleagues about the ideas suggested in this chapter:

1. How much merit is there is seeing narratives as conforming to predictable rules of configuration?
2. What benefit, if any, is there in helping students to construct a set of rules of configuration?
3. What learning activities would you design to help students to recognize what they already know about ways that narratives are configured and then express a set of rules of their own?

Chapter 7

Considering Competing Critical Views

It is hard to imagine a literature scholar commenting on a serious work of literature without an awareness and careful attention to the body of critical commentary about the work. In fact, as Graff (2009) has argued, it would be meaningless for the scholar to comment on the work of literature if the commentator was simply repeating the consensus view. With an awareness of competing critical views of a text, a reader can frame a problem that elevates the significance of the commentary. Furthermore, an awareness that there are competing critical views can provide the motivation for close reading, which probably means much rereading in this context.

In recalling his development as a reader of complex literary texts, Graff (1992) notes that his recognition that other readers disagreed about how to read and appraise a text spurred him to read the text more closely. Specifically, Graff (1992) notes that his instructor had made the class aware about disagreements about the ending of *The Adventures of Huckleberry Finn* and how Twain might have undermined the quality of the whole novel by having Huck revert to his pre-journey state:

> Having the controversy over the ending in mind, I now had some issues *to watch out for* as I read, issues that reshaped the way I read the earlier chapters as well as the later ones and focused my attention. And having issues to watch out for made it possible not only to concentrate, as I had not been able to do earlier, but to put myself in the text—to read with a sense of personal engagement that I had not felt before. (p. 68)

The language is noteworthy here: Graff was able to "put myself in the text" and had a "sense of personal engagement." In a sense, I might say that he had not really read the text until he was aware that others were reading the text in distinct ways and disagreed strongly in their assessments.

Perhaps in some enchanted high schools, without a teacher's prompting, students readily pore over complex texts and enter into Socratic dialogues about how they have constructed the meaning and assessed the esthetic merits of the work. Perhaps there are also schools in which an English teacher can assign students to read a body of literary criticism as well as the literary text and expect learners to enter into debates about the merits of the critics' commentaries. But such schools are hard to imagine. Instead, in most high schools, students often need a good deal of preparation and encouragement to read a complex literary text.

In any school, students are very bright and can grapple with competing critical arguments, although it is unlikely that a teacher would ask the learners to read mature criticism for which the critics assume certain knowledge about an author, the author's body of literature, and the language that scholars use for talking about abstract concepts. How, then, can a high school English teacher help students to become aware of the critical debates that surround a text, not as ancillary to the main event, but as a means for entering into the text and engaging with it personally?

FROM SIMPLE TO COMPLEX

As a basic principle for planning instruction, teachers would be wise to follow a sequence of activities that moves students from relatively simple tasks to more complex tasks. This can take the form of beginning with relatively simple texts and then progressing to more complex texts. Many teachers have experienced some success in working with picture books, particularly some works by Dr. Seuss and Shel Silverstein. Consider a high school librarian who fought many battles with community members who sought to remove certain texts from the library. This part of her profile marked her as someone who defended the right to experience many different kinds of texts, even those that some critics found dangerous or offensive. At the same time, the librarian read Shel Silverstein's *The Giving Tree* to her two young boys and then promptly removed it from the home library.

This experience reveals that the text might be a ready source of controversy, lending itself to an exploration of competing points of view about the implications of the narrative and the value of the ideas the author seems to promote. Of course, there has been a long, ongoing debate about its implications (Holmes and Galchen, 2014): Does the text celebrate sacrifice and selflessness out of love for another, or does it condemn selfishness and warn against the wholehearted service toward another? Is it a realistic, not moralistic, depiction of common human relationships, or is it a dangerous book that, as one online critic noted, "The Nazis would have loved."

Typically, high school students do not mind if their English teacher takes up some class time to read a children's book aloud and share the illustrations, as if it were story time at the library. Mostly, students are amused, and some students will remember having read the book earlier in their childhood. Perhaps the reading of the book by itself will prompt a lively discussion about the implications. An alternative is to frontload the reading—sort of priming the criticism pump to encourage a variety of views of the text.

Pichert and Anderson (1976) report that the prompts that focus the attention of readers influence what they recall and how they experience a text. Their research suggests that if a teacher prompts different readers in distinctly different ways *before* reading a text, the students are likely to construct distinctly different meanings and judge the merits of a text in a variety of different ways.

You will find below four prompts to lead to the reading of Silverstein's *The Giving Tree*. In classroom practice, the teacher would distribute the printed prompts randomly across the room and ask students to write a response to what they read: "Do you agree with the ideas expressed in the paragraph above? Why? Do you disagree with the ideas? Why?" As a rule, when students write a brief response, they seriously consider the extent to which they agree with the perspective. The idea is to prompt a critical debate and not to indoctrinate readers to a particular view. Writing an evaluation of the view helps learners to clarify their own perspective.

FOUR PRE-READING PROMPTS FOR *THE GIVING TREE*

1. If you consistently do favors and give gifts to other persons, eventually those other persons will begin to take you for granted and expect you always to be the one to pay, to give in, and to sacrifice. Although someone might consider your behavior generous, it is actually destructive because you hurt yourself and make others dependent.
2. The world is a better place because some kind persons are very generous. Of course, being generous means giving up something that you would value. If you give up things that are really of no value to you, you can hardly be considered generous. Although this kind of sacrifice might be difficult, generosity is a very important trait to develop as you grow older, and the children need to learn the importance of generosity when they are young.
3. Some selfish persons expect others to give them whatever they want. Selfish persons think so highly of themselves that they cannot imagine

someone not wanting to give them things. These selfish persons find it impossible to recognize the pain and difficulty of another person's sacrifice. The selfish person cannot put himself or herself in the place of the one making the sacrifice. Everyone will be at least little selfish at times, but you should learn to reduce your selfishness as you grow older.
4. The worst possible relationship occurs when one person is always giving and sacrificing and the other person is always wanting and taking. At first you would think these two persons are compatible, but actually the relationship is destructive for both. The person who constantly gives will lose self-esteem and feel that only the other person is worthy of comfort, satisfaction, and pleasure. The selfish person will come to expect the sacrifice of the other person and will take him or her for granted.

Our experience has been that after responding to these pre-reading prompts, students enter with their classmates into a critical discussion about the position Silverstein seems to advance, how they determined what Silverstein probably expected them to notice, and the broader implications of the story, including its illustrations. As you might expect, some students read the story as a celebration of generosity, even when the tree is reduced to a stump. Others criticize the behavior of the boy/man for his selfishness and insensitivity. Inevitably, some students will point out that the tree is depicted as female and the character she selflessly supports is male. When students notice what seems to be Silverstein's attention to this detail, they see an illustration of a broader societal pattern—with moms, wives, and girlfriends often expected to sacrifice their own interests, comforts, and general well-being to advance the preferences of a male.

Others will argue that the gender assignments are more or less random and such one-sided relationships occur between partners, friends, and family members, regardless of gender identity. This swirl of critical possibilities leaves discussion participants in the uneasy position of defending their own judgments and entertaining the possible merits in alternative positions. Fostering this area of doubt and arena of critical exchange is a healthy and productive way to talk about literature. Furthermore, learning to engage civilly and rationally with competing points of view, even when the focus is on a work of children's literature, prepares adolescents for participating in similar activities with more complex texts, as you will see later in this chapter.

Reacting to Prepared Critical Positions

While constructed statements can prepare learners for reading a text through a variety of lenses in order to reveal distinctive responses during discussion, more typically, readers consider the competing critical views *after* they have read the text. For mature students of literature, this would mean turning attention to published literary criticism, if such material exists for a selected work and is accessible. For high school students, however, it is a simple matter for the teacher to construct a few competing views.

To illustrate, consider Dr. Seuss's "Gertrude McFuzz," which appears in the collection titled *Yertle the Turtle and Other Stories* (1958). The narrative is simple: Gertrude, a girl bird, envies the beautiful tail feathers of another bird, named Lolla-Lee-Lou. When Gertrude appeals to her uncle, a doctor named Dake, he directs her to the pill-berry bush, where Getrude consumes one pill after another until she has a spectacular set of tail feathers. But the weight of all the new tail feathers prevents Gertrude from lifting into the air, and she has to be carried home by a flock of birds who "almost broke all their beaks" in an effort to support Gertrude. Then Getrude endures a long process of removing all the new tail feathers, returning her to her original condition.

In introducing this popular children's story to high school students, we follow up by asking them to evaluate the responses of two readers. The two responses allow us to pose a question that students often consider when their teachers ask them to write interpretations of literary texts: Is there a "right" answer? Here is a further question: If there is no verifiable "right" answer about interpretation, how can a teacher ever find fault with any student's interpretation? This is *the* classic question often articulated by scientists or other empirically oriented readers, and you can see some suggested responses below. The two views below prompt the critical commentary about the text.

WHO IS RIGHT?

Is There Any Truth to What These Readers Say?

Sally says this: The message of the book is that drugs are dangerous. Gertrude does not feel very good about herself because she has only one little tail feather. She is desperate to be like Lola-Lee-Lou. So, Gertrude takes pills from the pill-berry tree to help her grow another tail feather. But she doesn't stop with just one. In a way, she becomes *addicted* and takes all the pills until she has so many tail feathers that she can't move. This is like being controlled by some addicting drug. She is incapacitated and has to be carried home. In order to return to her old self, she has to have all the feathers removed in a very painful procedure. This is like going through detox. Finally, Gertrude learns her lesson that addicting drugs will not solve your problems; instead, they will cause more problems. This is what Dr. Seuss meant to say.

Bob offers this view: In this story, Dr. Seuss is suggesting that all women are very conceited and envious of others. Gertrude sees Lola-Lee-Lou and wants to have long, colorful tail feathers like her. Gertrude will do almost anything to get the kind of tail feathers she wants. This is like a woman who sees another woman with a particular style of clothing and will do almost anything to get it because she feels that she has to have it in order to feel special. Based on this story, I think that Dr. Seuss feels that all women are self-centered and conceited.

Felix concludes: I think that Dr. Seuss wanted to show kids that it is not a good idea to want something that you weren't born with. In other words, don't try to be something you're not. Gertrude wanted to have something that she admired in someone else because she wasn't satisfied with her own appearance. This kind of thing happens a lot with kids. They think they are too short or too tall or too skinny or too fat. Everyone is the way they are supposed to be. When you try to become something that is not natural, then you have problems like Gertrude did.

Typically, students have strong reactions to these responses to the story. As you can imagine, the discussions touch on several perennial critical considerations: What did the author *intend*? How can you figure this out? What does the author reveal, regardless of intention? If the author's attitude is a product of the historical moment when he was writing, can we hold him to a standard that seems more enlightened today? Must we read the text from the vantage point of the year in which it was composed? Is it fair to impose contemporary standards when constructing meaning and judging the merits of a story? The following composite discussion reveals how students typically talk about the reported responses from Sally, Bob, and Felix.

Ms. Caputo: What do you think about Sally's commentary? Does it have any merit?

Carlos: Well, it is logical. I mean, she puts a bunch of details together. Getrude eats pills, and they were prescribed by a doctor. But she took too many. But that's not becoming addicted to like an opioid. She got what she wanted, but she got too much of what she wanted. When was this story written?

Ms. Caputo: The copyright is 1958.

Carlos: Oh, so there. In 1958, there wasn't an opioid crisis. There wasn't any like "say no to drugs" campaign.

Sara: I agree. Dr. Seuss couldn't have been thinking about an anti-drug answer. It's a children's story! He wouldn't be telling kids not to take drugs. I think he was just telling kids that they shouldn't be like envious of other people, you know, like kids do.

Ms. Caputo: But, clearly, Getrude is taking too many *pills* in an attempt to get what she wants. As Carlos says, it does seem logical: there is textual evidence to support an anti-drug message in the story.

Marcos: Yeah, it's logical, but you can find evidence to support just about anything. Dr. Seuss might be warning kids that you're not supposed to find easy ways to get what you want because you are envious of someone else. So, I think the message is bigger than an anti-drug warning. I think he is warning kids about trying to find easy ways to change themselves. He wants them to feel good about the way they are.

Ms. Caputo: Does that make any sense? I mean, if that is a central message, does it make sense to encourage kids to be satisfied with who they are? We all try to improve ourselves in one way or another. It is scary to think of a world where everyone is complacent and does not seek to improve.

Caitlyn: I don't read the story like you are not supposed to improve yourself. Everybody tries to make themselves better. They want to look better or do better in school to go to good colleges and stuff. But it is like shaming people because of their body shape or because they don't fit an image of the way you're supposed to be. I think the story tells kids that they are good the way they are, even if they don't fit someone else's image.

This is a brief example from a longer exchange in which students evaluated all three of the views that the teacher shared. The three views do not represent distinct critical theories, but they do offer many students an alternative view of the story, which prompts readers to reevaluate their own assumptions and to assess the validity of the expressed response. Students take into account the time period when Seuss composed the story in order to infer his possible intentions.

Some students are likely to compare "Getrude McFuzz" to other works by the same author, which allows them to check for consistency in what they judge to be his sentiments. So, they look to the immediate text and compare it to other texts with which they are familiar. Those students who remain Dr. Seuss fans recoil at Bob's suggestion that Seuss was a misogynist who found fault with women for what he saw as an inclination toward vanity and envy. Bob's reading of the story makes some students uncomfortable, especially when he can point to a pattern in the text that would reveal a kind of bias against women.

As Graff (1992) reports from his own experience, this provocation and discomfort prompt readers to invest themselves in looking more closely at the text. There are many children's stories, including familiar fairy tales, that a class can approach in a similar way, with the intention of immersing learners in the process of constructing meaning and comparing their own interpretations with those of others, especially others who offer unexpected alternatives. Again, the practice with the reading and related critical conversations about a simple text positions students to tackle more complex texts in similar ways.

Building on Practice

In this sequence moving from simple to complex, consider now a story often anthologized for high school readers. What are we to make of Kurt

Vonnegut's "Harrison Bergeron"? The futuristic tale reports that it is 2081 and a Handicapper General has directed an effort to make everyone equal in all regards—no one exceptional in intelligence, creativity, or physical endowments. For a brief moment one exceptional person, Harrison, tears off his handicaps and declares himself as the new ruling monarch, accompanied by a willing empress. Of course, the Handicapper General manages to suppress this mutiny.

A teacher might assign the reading of the story by admitting that she finds the story puzzling: Is it an argument in support of monarchy? Does Vonnegut embrace the notion that societies develop through a process of survival of the fittest? Does the story reveal Vonnegut as an opponent of equality? Is Vonnegut longing for a world where dominant males rule dominions? While not reviewing several critical theories that could apply to reading literature in general (cf. Applemen, 2015; Gillespie, 2010), a teacher could ask adolescents to consider that several readers can have distinct views about a work of literature.

For the sake of fostering deep critical dives into "Harrison Bergeron," students might evaluate four critical responses that one could label *political, gendered, psychological,* and *historical/biographical,* but you don't need these labels and can share reactions as *View 1, View 2, View 3,* and *View 4*. These views derive from a body of literary criticism about Vonnegut in general and "Harrison Bergeron" specifically (see, for example, Hattenhauer, 1998; Reed, 2000; Schatt, 1976). Here are four possibilities, but teachers can invent their own, perhaps extending possibilities for viewing the text.

FOUR VIEWS OF VONNEGUT'S "HARRISON BERGERON"

View 1: There are three female characters in the story: Harrison's mom, who is as "normal" as can be; a ballerina possessed of beauty and graceful athleticism; and Diana Moon Glampers, an agent of suppression and cruelty. In contrast, the two featured male characters are distinctive because of their power and intelligence, revealed by the extent of their imposed handicaps. While the story is satirical, Vonnegut reveals that in his view of the normal, unimpeded course of society, the naturally dominant males would be the great thinkers and therefore the natural rulers. In this worldview, women take either a subordinate role (e.g., housewife or the selected empress) or a twisted managerial role, eliminating the apparently threatening male.

View 2: While some readers might judge that Vonnegut argues for an unrestrictive competitive society, his history as a writer and political thinker is decidedly left of center. He was critical about the way that television dominated popular culture, moving the population toward a regretful mediocrity. As a writer and consumer of culture, he supported the arts and argued for greater government support of the arts. Considering Vonnegut's own background, a reader can interpret the satire as an argument against a mediocrity that threatens Americans because of lack of government support for the arts and a harmful contentment with popular forms of entertainment such as television. Given Vonnegut's history, the only way to read the story is as an argument against misconceptions about the political concept of *equality* and an argument for supporting the exceptionalities that benefit all Americans.

View 3: Either Vonnegut was confused about what he wanted to say with his story, or he was intentionally arguing for an autocratic state in which the obviously gifted should rule over the weaker and the less intelligent. Vonnegut appears to regret communities that reward people for their "participation," just as Harrison's mother recommends a raise for the television announcer who tried his best. The story opens with the report that the United States has finally realized equality in all things. This obviously impossible exaggeration suggests that Vonnegut scoffs at the idea of striving toward equality. He must recognize that as a popular and best-selling writer, he is exceptional, both in the production of his work and in the wealth and influence he has attained. As a distinctive writer, he is not the equal of every other American. He cannot imagine anyone handicapping the literary artist, nor any other exceptional human being. As a "natural law" or "self-evident truth," perhaps the rule of the exceptional seems to Vonnegut to be the appropriate political arrangement, as long as everyone is equal before God and the law.

View 4: The story reveals that Vonnegut is conflicted about the way he understands the concept of *equality*. On the one hand, it is hard to imagine that Vonnegut would not respect the idea that all humans are created equal. But what does that mean to him? The preposterous situation in "Harrison Bergeron" is that a government official manages to make everyone equally mediocre. In poking fun at this notion, Vonnegut acknowledges that there are distinctions among people—that we are not equal in all ways. The story depicts the possibility of handicapped dancers, musicians, and television announcers as a crazy notion; we would celebrate that there are exceptional people in these fields, as well as exceptional leaders, philosophers, academicians, and athletes. Open competition allows for exceptional individuals to reach heights in their professions—the prima ballerina, the starting quarterback, the endowed professor, the elected government official. But taken to an extreme, as

Vonnegut demonstrates with Harrison Bergeron defeating his restraints and declaring himself Emperor, the most intelligent, physically gifted, and pulchritudinous would naturally become the ruler, and it would be a horrible tragedy to see such giftedness destroyed. The notion of *equality* as a political ideal and promise has escaped us for hundreds of years, and Vonnegut reveals his own struggle to realize the balance between treating all people as equals in order to guarantee justice and celebrating and protecting exceptionality.

Just as university students might read a literary work first and then compare their readings to the commentary from published scholars, high school students can read the story and then consider diverse responses. The four views above can help to prompt students to consider several possibilities, which in turn can influence them to react with their own synthesized interpretations. There are two likely instructional formats, both relying on small group discussion. First, a teacher can organize several small groups and then assign each group a specific view to apply to the story, evaluate its merits, and then share the group's conclusions with the rest of the class. This process would expose the whole class to several possibilities, helping each student to sort out a reasoned interpretation in the face of the competing viewpoints.

The second possibility is to form groups and share all four (or as many as you can construct) views with each of the teams. The group task would be to judge the relative merits of the views and prepare to share with the class how they determined that a view was reasonable and others were less reasonable. An appropriate expectation would be that each contributor to the small group discussion and the large group sharing would be able to cite textual evidence (what you noticed and how you were able to construct meaning) to support an analysis. Again, the sharing would expose students to many possibilities for viewing and judging the story, involving all students in the procedures for analysis.

Extending Practice

Earlier work (McCann and Flanagan, 2002; Graff, 2003) reports how groups of high school students considered critical conflicts as part of their experience with a Shakespeare play. In preparing ninth graders for reading *The Tempest*, teachers distributed "postcards" to students, with the messages ostensibly written by characters on the island of Sycorax. Over several days, students received a different postcard per day, with each student receiving messages from a single character, one who attempts to curry sympathy from the reader. Here are examples from Caliban and from Prospero:

SAMPLE "POSTCARDS" FROM THE ISLAND OF SYCORAX

Message 1 from Caliban:
Friend,
My life is complete misery. I am a slave. Do you know what it is to lose your liberty, to have choices, freedom of movement, right of protest, all taken away from you? I live now only to serve the relentless tyrant Prospero. He makes me do all his menial chores. I collect wood, day and night, not because he <u>needs</u> wood, but because he wishes to exercise his <u>power</u> over me. There is no end in sight for my suffering.
Regards,
Caliban

Message 2 from Caliban:
Friend,
It is so unfair that I have to work as a slave on an island where I should be a king. You remember that my mother owned and ruled this island. She is dead now and cannot use her magic powers to protect me. Prospero, a visitor, a guest in my homeland, has taken ownership of everything and expects me to obey him. It is <u>so</u> unfair.
Regards,
Caliban

Message 1 from Prospero:
Dear Friend:
I continue to make the best of my difficult circumstances on the island. As you know, I was once the leader of an advanced society; but my villainous brother drove me from my position. I was left with only my infant daughter, and I've labored for many years to make a safe home for the two of us. I no longer know comfort, polite company, and the finer qualities of a cultured society. But I will survive to bring some light of civilization into this dark corner of the world.
Sincerely,
Prospero

Message 2 from Prospero:
Dear Friend:
It is difficult to find good help these days. There is a detestable slave on the island. His name is Caliban. He is an ignorant and potentially violent primitive inhabitant. I have done all that I could do to educate him and to train him to be a polite and productive contributor to society. I have attempted to raise him

out of the mud and mire. I have even shared my personal dwelling with him. How does he thank me? He tried to violate my innocent daughter! He habitually complains about doing simple tasks! He is lazy, ignorant, and evil! I must always be on my guard.

Sincerely,
Prospero

Other postcards arrived from Ariel, Miranda, Ferdinand, and Gonzalo. Before reading the play, teachers were able to ask the students what they knew about the story based on what a character had told them. As you might imagine, the students became sympathetic toward someone who was overtly soliciting their sympathy. In sharing the story, students began disputing each other about the nature of the characters, their sense of victimhood, their sense of justice and of justice violated, their values, their inclinations, and their conflicts and complexities. This sharing and exchange put students in a position to read the play critically, initially looking for support for their views of the characters and then reshaping their thinking as they experienced more and more of the play.

The postcards *introduced* the play, but teachers also exposed students to a more detailed written critique of the play as a means for *reflecting* on what the class had experienced. Teachers collaborated in writing critical reviews of *The Tempest* in the form of book reviews. As Graff and Phelan (2002) document in their edition of the play, there is a long critical history about the play, including more recent postcolonial readings. One could label the views the teachers constructed as *gendered, political, historical/biographical,* and *psychological*. The labels are less important than the fact that the reviews are distinct and encourage students to see the play through various lenses. Here is one example:

A STORM OF RESISTANCE

The Politics of Power and Colonization

To any sensitive reader it should be clear who the hero is in William Shakespeare's latest book, *The Tempest*. While smug royalty sit upon their thrones in Europe and delight in imperial expansion, brave men and women throughout the world resist exploitation and oppression. Caliban, the most intriguing character in the book, is one of these courageous rebels. He gallantly resists the rule of Prospero and enjoys the freedom of spirit and the power of will, even though he is forced into slavery.

The story begins with Prospero, the former despotic and negligent ruler of Milan, using his considerable powers to start a storm that threatens the lives of the crew and passengers upon a passing ship. All on board, privileged class and the proletarian workers alike, share equally in the threat of a watery death. While everyone aboard panics, Prospero confidently wields all the power in a personal plot to reclaim political control in Europe. Prospero pays little attention to the pain or sorrows of others: his own goals and schemes are his only concern. He uses everyone as a pawn—the sailors, the ship's passengers, the inhabitants of the island, and even his own daughter.

Given Shakespeare's track record, it appears that he *unwittingly* demonstrates that the imperialist leaders of the world concern themselves only with material gains and the extension of power. Which of the European rulers can we respect in this story? Antonio takes control of power away from his own brother, caring little for the welfare of the former Duke or his daughter. Alonso, the King of Naples, conspires with Antonio in the hope of extending his power. Stephano and Trinculo follow the example of their leaders and make a foolhardy attempt at assuming rule of the island. Caliban alone never succumbs completely to the threats of Prospero. The perpetual resistance to the unjust exercise of power is the only effective weapon against encroachment.

So the book becomes *Caliban's story*, and his history is the history of colonization. When Prospero and Miranda arrive on Caliban's island, the land where his mother once ruled, Caliban welcomes them gladly. He shows them the resources of the island, without which they could not survive. All of Prospero's frivolous study and scholarly pretensions prove useless in a new environment. He must depend on Caliban, whose language, tastes, and manners are perfectly adapted to the island. However, as soon as Prospero learns from Caliban, he thanks his selfless savior by enslaving him. Prospero follows his European model and proclaims himself the ruler of the island, lord of all the inhabitants. The basis for his claim is the power he has to destroy those who challenge him.

The title of the book, *The Tempest*, is an apt metaphor for the continuous state of revolt that is necessary to overcome the bitter rule of arrogant leaders who wish to colonize a "new world," that is, a world that is new to the invaders. Caliban sustains his own tempest—the storm of revolt—in the constant resistance to domination. Unlike the subservient and sniveling Ariel, the noble Caliban never surrenders entirely. While Ariel pleads for freedom, Caliban demands his rights. While Ariel executes Prospero's insidious schemes, Caliban plots the forcible overthrow of the tyrant. Ariel pleads and awaits Prospero's will. Caliban resists and acts, until he is finally rewarded when the invaders withdraw to their petty fiefdoms.

This book is a dangerous one: dangerous if the reader is fooled into seeing Prospero as a noble sage and able leader; dangerous to the world's plotting despots who might face a storm of resistance from the true nobility of the lands they hope to devour.

This kind of review simplifies matters a bit for students who may be unfamiliar with a postcolonial view of the play or any literature. But in high school, teachers are not grooming literary scholars; they are fostering the enthusiastic and critical reading of literature. The other views—ones that might be labeled *gendered, political, historical/biographical,* and *psychological*—offer distinct ways of reading the play and evaluating the characters. As students enter discussions about the play, they also assess the merits of the alternative ways of looking at the play. As we discuss in greater detail in chapter 8, when students are aware of competing views, they have a means for framing a critical problem that they can address in their written responses.

YOUR VIEW

This chapter makes the case for exposing students to a variety of critical views of a text without formal teaching of critical theory and introducing technical terminology associated with critical theories. The chapter offers ways of injecting the study of literature with conflict prompted by considering competing ways of looking at a text. At the same time, while a teacher should be aware of a genuine critical tradition associated with a text, high school students are not likely to gain much from reading most literary criticism. It is enough that learners are aware that different readers read the same text in different, and sometimes contradictory, ways. With your colleagues, you might want to discuss these questions:

1. Given the many demands on a high school teacher of English, how realistic is it that teachers will prepare for the teaching of a literary text by also reading selected criticism of the text?
2. How viable is it for teachers to plan together for the teaching of a work of literature by discussing the several critical lenses through which to view the text?
3. If you would formally teach students aspects of critical theory, as Appleman suggests, how would you approach such an effort?
4. If your job as an English teacher is *not* to prepare future literature scholars, how useful is it to attempt to engage students in discussions about competing critical views when it might be enough simply to influence students to read the assigned text?

Chapter 8

Responding to Literature

Perhaps a common conception of an English class envisions literature as the core element in the curriculum and discussion of the literature as an almost daily occurrence. If you were to visit a typical high school English class, you might observe a classroom interchange that looks something like this:

Ms. Browmeier: So, why does Montresor seek revenge against Fortunato?
Paul: It says that Fortunato hurt him a "thousand times."
Ms. Browmeier: How has he hurt him?
Paul: It doesn't say. Maybe he cheated him or insulted him or something.
Ms. Browmeier: OK, so Montresor wanted revenge because Fortunato has hurt him in some way and has insulted him. What season of the year is it?
Loretta: I'm not sure. Is it winter? It's kind of cold, and I think Fortunato is sick with a cold.
Ms. Browmeier: Yes, but what holiday season is it?
Loretta: I don't know. Like Christmas or New Year?
Ms. Browmeier: Anyone else?
Paul: It says it was a spring night when they met on the street.
Ms. Browmeier: Well, it's carnival season: you know, like Mardi Gras. People dress in costume and party. That's an important detail. So how does Montresor trick Fortunato into following him into the vaults? Carlo, how about you?
Carlo: Well, the guy is kind of drunk already and he tells him he has this really great wine and the guy can't resist.
Paul: Montresor knows that Fortunato thinks he's an expert about wine, so Montresor plays on his pride. He even gives him chances to turn back, like he is sort of teasing him.
Ms. Browmeier: This is a form of torment, isn't it?

Such exchanges occur repeatedly, both in high schools and at the university. Nystrand (1997) would characterize this as *recitation*. The questions are not "authentic" because they have pre-specified answers. Perhaps such exchanges are necessary occasionally, and to a degree, for the teacher to assess quickly how students have comprehended the story, or whether they have read it at all. At the same time, the students' brief responses do not amount to rich and elaborated responses to a literary text, and the exchanges do not support students very much in making complex inferences about the text and evaluating the implications. An actual discussion would expose students to multiple possibilities for judging the implications of the story, which, in turn, would support learners in writing responses about the story.

Students can respond to literature in a variety of meaningful ways: through visual representations, through film interpretations, through their own stories and poems, and even through interpretive dance. But the common modes of response in school are discussions and written analyses. These are two broad and complex subjects. Each deserves book-length attention (see, for example, Johannessen et al., 2008; McCann et al., 2018; see also H. Smith, 2015). Unmistakably, there is value in talking to others about the literature that we read, especially when the discussion moves beyond recitation and involves several perspectives on how to make meaning from the text.

Certainly, literature scholars pay close attention to what others have to say about the works of literature that are the focus of their scholarship, even when they vehemently disagree with some commentary. Unless teachers are assured of their infallibility, they have to admit to gaining much from the insights of others, and even the views with which teachers disagree put them in the position to explain, if only to themselves, why they disagree and why they cling to their own contested views. And, as suggested later in this chapter, students' extensive involvement in sustained and substantive discussions about a text positions the learners to write elaborated analyses.

The goal of this chapter is to identify practices that promote classroom discussions about literature and to suggest some general approaches to writing about literature. The previous chapters discuss how to prepare learners for their reading of complex texts and how to develop some facility with making complex inferences about the texts. In the end, as a means for fostering deep understanding and appreciation, teachers will want students to respond in discussions and writing; these forms of responses also provide the overt behavior that allow a teacher to assess students' growth and their command of the procedures for interpreting and evaluating complex literary texts. The teacher of literature needs to know how to initiate, sustain, and connect meaningful discussions of literature, and the teacher needs to know how to prepare students to write about complex texts in a mature, logical, and coherent way.

SOME RUDIMENTS OF DISCUSSIONS OF LITERATURE

Much of our classroom methodology, and what we have tried to teach in Methods classes, has depended on discussion, especially discussion about literature. Sometimes these discussions have been frustrating efforts to inspire students to speak about how they have interpreted a work of literature or about their judgments about the author's implications. As teachers become more aware of the conditions and responses that foster open discussion, the more fruitful and satisfying the discussions will become for everyone involved.

Discussion can be small group collaborations or whole class deliberations. A teacher should be aware of some rudiments of whole class discussion. Below, you will find some general guidelines (also see Textbox 8.2) for whole class discussion, followed by examples of how these practices look in action in the classroom.

Before reviewing the pedagogical moves involved in facilitating discussion, consider the obvious reality that no one in a group will want to participate in a conversation in which they are trying out ideas and advancing tentative understandings in a condition of animosity and incivility. This holds true both for offline conversations and online discussions. A teacher might impose rules for civil conversation, but it is most impactful to discuss what students expect of their partners in collaborations and discussions. If you ask students to jot down three or four expectations for others and themselves, the shared list will reveal common ground that can serve as the class norms that everyone can invoke when necessary. Textbox 8.1 below offers an example of the norms for discussion in one class.

Class Norms for Discussion and Collaboration

- Respond to each other respectfully, especially when topics are sensitive or controversial. In this context, *respectfully* means no aggressive stances, no insults, no dismissive reactions, and so on.
- Allow and encourage diverse points of view.
- Listen actively to partners.
- Encourage and don't suppress participation from everyone, both in conversation and in completing elements of a project.
- Don't talk over others, and don't dominate the conversation.
- Check periodically for agreement or common understanding, even when the understanding is that there isn't agreement.
- Respond honestly, without being brutally candid, even if that honesty might make you feel a bit uncomfortable.

Typically, a teacher will come to class equipped with a set of questions to prompt discussion. Authentic questions are useful, but it is most powerful to frame genuine interpretive problems or note how readers have disagreed about how to read or value a work of literature. It would be refreshing for the students to hear the teacher say something like this:

> You know, I have read this story at least a dozen times and I still can't figure out who the narrator is. I know that the story came from a science fiction magazine, but if the narrator is supposed to be an alien creature, I have to shrug and say "So what?" If the narrator is a human child, then I am puzzled about how it can do what it claims it can do.

While many teachers are hesitant to reveal that they have trouble understanding some aspect of the literature that they have assigned to read, the rich conversations that mature readers have about literature, both in person and in academic journals, most often involve areas of doubt or disagreement. Who would want to participate in a conversation in which the participants simply share their agreements and enthusiasms? Such conversations do not have to be agonistic, especially if the participants approach their discussion with an appreciation that their sharing and evaluation of arguments (in the sense of logical units of thought) can enrich and advance their understandings.

When a teacher introduces a problem or area of doubt as the focus for discussion, the conversation can move in any of a variety of directions. This means that a teacher will have to anticipate the possibilities and be flexible enough to engage in the discussion along any path that promises to help everyone to have a deeper understanding of a text and richer assessment of its craft and implications. The list in textbox 8.2 suggests some useful practices. Below the list, we discuss and illustrate these practices.

Rudiments of Whole Class Discussion

- Frame genuine interpretive problems.
- Allow time for students to prepare.
- Listen carefully to a student's response and paraphrase often.
- Ask appropriate follow-up questions.
- Invite other students to respond to each other.
- Summarize a series of exchanges.
- Assess the impact of discussion.
- Connect discussion as part of an ongoing conversation.

Discussion among literature scholars do not amount to reiterating common understanding and sharing enthusiasms about texts. More likely, the scholars are talking about the areas of doubt and disagreement regarding how to read and evaluate a text. In other words, the discussants are grappling with problems and perhaps debating about areas of disagreement. While many scholars seem to take delight in intellectual combat, the more productive discussions serve the purposes of sharing knowledge and testing ideas. In this context, a discussant might say to a challenger, "Thank you for disagreeing." While this might sound strange to anyone who disdains disagreement, the testing of our arguments serves the important function of moving us beyond reciting our prejudice and forces us to refine our position and consider other possibilities.

Many teachers lament when discussions fall flat. These failed discussions are most often recitations with students who may not have read, or they are a teacher's efforts to lead students down a path to the understanding or evaluation that the teacher endorses. A possible alternative to this frustrating experience involves providing students with a purpose for reading by framing an interpretive problem or revealing an apparent and genuine conflict about how to interpret and evaluate the text.

But no one will be eager to jump into the conversation without sufficient opportunity to collect thoughts and prepare analyses. So, the first suggestion is to provide students enough time to think about the problem that will be the focus for discussion and allow them to prepare their contributions to the conversation. For many teachers, this might be a time spent with students writing a few notes in a journal. Perhaps after this period of written reflection, students will join partners in small groups to share what they have written.

The whole class discussion might begin with the teacher reiterating the problem or general prompt. Some teachers prefer to circle the desks rather than have desks in rows, but this is less important than having an authentic interpretive problem as the focus for discussion and cultivating a supportive environment for dialogue and including as many students as possible in the conversation.

After you initiate discussion, listen carefully to a student's response and paraphrase it rather than evaluate it. If the discourse is in fact recitation, then the teacher will be listening for correct answers and the evaluative responses will signal to the class that the "discussion" is a game of guessing the answers that the teacher wants to hear. This is quite different from the kind of dialogue that explores and evaluates possibilities for reading characters, judging their behavior, inferring thematic implications, responding to these implications, and so on.

Discussions are opportunities for students to develop their critical thinking about literature. Critical thinking means more than asserting any conclusion that comes to mind. In fact, as students engage with each other, we would like to see evidence of critical thinking—that speakers can support claims, not just by pointing to some passage in a text, but also by citing some principles about how narratives work, how humans behave, how we know that symbols mean what we claim they mean. In other words, students should be both citing passages from the text and invoking various *rules* for constructing meaning, rules that they may have derived from the kind of activities illustrated in chapters 4 and 5.

Ask appropriate follow-up questions to invite students to elaborate on their responses. These follow-up questions do not need to sound combative, but should recognize the basic expectations for expressing logical arguments. The two recurring questions should be *Why?* (Why do you make that assertion?) and *So what?* (So what if you point to a passage of the text? How does that passage or other "data" support your claim?). The kind of informal reasoning that these questions prompt align with Toulmin (1958/2003) rather than with syllogistic reasoning.

If the discussion is to be genuinely dialogic, you will want students to talk to each other and not filter all responses through the teacher. An alternative to the common reflex of offering evaluative responses to students' contributions is to paraphrase what students have said and then invite other students to evaluate their peers' observations or arguments respectfully. If you are concerned about encouraging students by providing positive feedback (or positive reinforcement in behaviorist terms), then be reassured that the paraphrase of a student's response is positive in itself, because it affirms the contribution is worthy of everyone's attention.

The effort to paraphrase accurately forces the teacher to strive to attend closely to what a student is saying and allows the speaker to correct the teacher who misrepresents the student's observations and analyses. Smagorinsky and Fly (1993) remind us that what a teacher does in facilitating discussion with the whole becomes a powerful model for how students should function when they move into small groups for discussion.

Since discussions about complex works of literature can require attention for an entire class meeting or across several class meetings, the teacher should take care from time to time to summarize a series of exchanges to highlight points of agreement and to identify remaining areas of doubt. Imagine an ongoing discussion about *Romeo and Juliet*. After 20 minutes of discussion, a teacher might say something like this:

> So far, I see that there remains disagreement about the extent to which adolescents need to obey the wishes of their parents. It seems to me that this class generally agrees that we need to be respectful of our parents' wishes, especially if we are living in their home and they are supporting us in many ways. But for many of you, this obligation might end when it comes to matters of the heart,

especially when your parents presume to arrange who you will marry. And—correct me if I am wrong—we still are unsure where Shakespeare stands on this question, even though he has been both son and father.

When discussions are extensive and widely exploratory, students feel grounded in hearing this kind of status report that reminds them about where they have been and where they still need to travel.

As an extension of any internal summary, a teacher will want to connect a discussion during one class meeting to other preceding discussions. At the same time, a teacher will likely want to project how the current discussion will prepare the learners for subsequent activities—perhaps by identifying a focus for the next reading or by practicing the intellectual moves that will be necessary for writing about the text currently under consideration.

If a teacher has a purpose for discussion as a means for responding to literature, that teacher will want to assess the efficacy of the classroom interchanges in meeting such a learning target. How does the discussion reveal that students have read the text? How does the discussion reveal that students are able to construct logical arguments to advance their interpretation and assessment of a text? How does the discussion reveal that students can adequately represent alterative views and assess those views honestly and respectfully?

Most commonly, teachers dream up point systems to award students for their participation in discussion, but such a system only tallies the instances when students have uttered something relevant during the classroom exchanges. Certainly some students are skilled at gaming the system by contributing often, even if they have not read the text nor have thought carefully about it. Some teachers might find themselves too inadequate as bookkeepers to be able to listen closely to students' contributions, orchestrating the exchanges across a class of eager participants, and then mark on a class roster each instance when student has said something.

Practitioners can learn much from high school teachers Dawn Forde and Andy Bouque (Forde, 2019; Bouque and Forde, 2019), who take care from time to time to record and transcribe what was said during class discussion. They can review parts of the transcript with the class to highlight and label the students' intellectual moves: that is, practicing uptake, citing evidence, applying rules to interpret evidence, evaluating a rebuttal position, and so on. Such demonstrations reveal to students the usefulness of the discussions and reassure students about their competence in contributing to discussions. In the end, if teachers are honest with themselves, they can check such transcripts to see if they are actually dominating discussion and to check if the discussions are serving as means for students to respond to literature in a meaningful way.

Discussions can take a number of forms and ideally students become confident enough to manage the discussions themselves. The notes above offer only the rudiments of facilitating class discussion. Nystrand (1997), McCann, et al. (2006), and McCann, et al. (2018) are useful resources for learning more about fostering productive dialogue in the classroom, especially in service of learning how to interpret literature and respond to texts logically.

DIALOGUE, ILLUSTRATED

As discussed in chapter 3, teachers can help students to engage with a text by preparing them with a problem related to the interpretation of the text or an evaluation of its implications. In the case of "A Cask of Amontillado," a teacher might frontload the reading with a discussion about the concept of revenge, including weighing the relative virtues of revenge versus mercy. Such an anticipatory discussion can prepare students for engaging extensively in matters of how to interpret the story and react to Poe's implications. Then, when it is time to discuss the story, the teacher can begin at the end of the story, noting that Montressor sought his revenge against Fortunato as a means to satisfy himself that Fortunato had paid for his harms and offenses. Here is how such a discussion might play out.

Ms. Whitney: At the beginning of the story, Montressor tells us that he means to realize revenge against Fortunato. If Montressor accomplishes his goal, Poe seems to be endorsing revenge, and this is a strange story to be reading in a school where you can get in trouble for fighting back against someone who is bullying you. Do you think Poe is using the story to show us that revenge can be a very satisfying act?

Janey: Well, yeah, because he like bricks the guy into a wall. That's terrible, but there's nobody to stop him, and probably no one will find out. So, it's like Poe is saying this is a good way to get back at your enemy.

Daric: But, in the end, Montressor is not totally satisfied. I think he wanted Fortunato to cry and plead for mercy or scream or something. So, he's not satisfied that Fortunato knew that Montressor was killing him for all the bad stuff that Fortunato did to him.

Silvia: He says something here. Wait. Here: "My heart grew sick; it must have been the cold." He is like trying to make an excuse that he feels sick because it is cold, but he might be feeling sick because he has just killed someone, and killed him in this really bad way.

Denyse: Well, if you killed someone, unless you are really a cold-blooded murderer, you would probably feel sick, too. But he is sort of satisfied that he killed him. I don't think he liked not having the guy cry out more.

Daric: Yeah, like in a lot of movies, the killer wants the victim to plead for mercy and know that this is pay-back. But the guy inside the wall stops replying. What's that supposed to mean?

Silvia: He stops talking because it is like he doesn't want to give him the satisfaction of knowing that he is scared and, you know, like pleading for his life.

Louis: Look, before that, he laughs.

Ms. Whitney: Who laughs?

Louis: The guy in the wall, Fortunato, right? It says, "a low laugh that erected the hairs upon my head." So that's like he is trying to laugh it off, hoping it is a joke. But his laugh actually scares Montressor.

Ms. Whitney: All right, I am getting confused. Is Poe, the author, recommending revenge or is he showing that it is a bad idea.

Daric: He is just showing this scary scene. Like, what could be worse than getting bricked up into a wall? I don't think he has to warn anyone about bricking your enemy inside a wall.

Christina: Who is he talking to anyhow? There's no one with him, so he is like confessing to us. Who is he supposed to be talking to?

Denyse: At the beginning, it says, "You, who knows so well the nature of my soul." So maybe he is supposed to be talking to a friend. Or maybe he is like confessing to a priest. That's who would know his soul. Maybe he is like at the end of his life and wants to confess.

Louis: So, if he is confessing, he knows he did something bad. He feels bad about it and has to tell it to someone. That's how Poe wrote it, to show in the end that revenge is a bad thing.

Ms. Whitney: That it is always a bad thing, or just in this instance when the killing is so horrible?

Louis: I don't know. He's telling us not to brick someone up into a wall. I don't know if he would think it would be bad to play a practical joke or something as revenge.

This discussion could easily begin in small groups and extend across a whole class and go on for much of a class meeting. In the end, the teacher is not prompting the students to recall details from the story for the sake of being able to produce a summary. Instead, the teacher poses an overarching critical question, and students inevitably point to details as they attempt to support their conclusions. The bit of dialogue above illustrates a class grappling together with a question about the implications of the story.

As suggested in earlier chapters, at least two intellectual moves are at work here: students are noticing elements in the text and they are drawing from their knowledge of how narratives in general work and how specific genres work and their understanding of human behavior to construct meaning from the details. The teacher is not leading the class down the path to a preconceived notion about what Poe was up to. Instead, the teacher admits to some confusion, perhaps from the ambiguities that Poe intentionally and artfully crafted into the narrative.

First, as a general rule, discussion is preferable to recitation, even if you have to ask students to recall some specifics about the text. If, ultimately, you want students to learn how to read critically, then you need to pose authentic critical questions and allow for genuine dialogue about those questions. If you want students to write critical analyses of texts, then you have to introduce actual critical problems and the discussions about texts should immerse students in the elements that can transfer to a written response: summarize, cite textual evidence to support claims, apply "rules" for reading literature as warrants for interpreting the details from the text, and identify and evaluate alternative interpretations and assessments.

FOSTERING WRITTEN RESPONSES TO LITERATURE

Gerald Graff (2009), in his usual provocative way, points out the "Unbearable Pointlessness of Literature Writing Assignments." The title suggests that teachers might forget about asking students to write about literature. Graff sums up his stance: "My quarrel with the standard classroom literature essay is summed up in the characterization of it I just offered: pseudoargument" (p. 8). At the same time, he insists that expressing and evaluating argument is at the core of learning: "I've made the case that argument—the dialectical clash of ideas—needs to be at the center of education" (p. 8).

Graff's concern is that in many contexts, students are either repeating what they judge the teacher wants to hear (e.g., Atticus Finch is a heroic character, or the Younger family has been foully treated by homeowners), or the writing assignment calls on students to take up predictable analytical frameworks (e.g., pattern of coming of age or a contrast between good and evil, light and dark, and so on) to the point where students could write and submit something without actually reading a text carefully or at all.

Some instructional principles are self-evident (and supported by research): that in order to write about *Romeo and Juliet*, for example, readers must have *read the play*, thought about its implications, and be aware of the problem-based conversations about the play. To be in a position to write meaningfully about the play, learners should have engaged frequently in the *procedures for analysis and argument* that can transfer to writing. In addition, readers must be aware of a genuine problem about the interpretation and/or evaluation of a text. This problem derives from a long critical tradition or has emerged recently as contemporary readers have assumed previously unfamiliar approaches to reading the text. As Graff points out, if there is no problem, then an elaborated written response is pointless, because it simply reiterates what has been said before.

As an introduction to the reading, a teacher should note authentic interpretive problems that are part of a long tradition or have emerged more recently. Framing of a critical problem is not likely to narrow students' possibilities for reading the text. In fact, it is unlikely that adolescents, who are still relative novices at studying literary texts, will, if unimpeded, discover some wholly innovative ways for looking at the text. Given the many responsibilities that students have during high school, it would be a rare student who would read a text more than once. It is only fair, then, for the teacher to alert students about an ongoing focus for discussion and about the substantial problem that can be a focus for writing about the text.

As noted earlier in this chapter, discussions should immerse students in the processes that are important to reading and writing. If the questions that are supposed to prompt discussion have pre-specified answers and are supposed to lead learners down the path to the teacher's understanding about the text, don't count on much participation and don't expect the discussions to position students to write in any meaningful and elaborated way about the text.

In contrast, if ongoing discussions focus on the problems related to interpreting the text and evaluating the implications, students will be in a position to offer their conclusions, supported by their attention to the features of the text and their explicit citation of "rules" for how to read literary texts. In addition, if discussion includes a variety of competing arguments about interpretations and evaluations, then students will be involved in assessing the merits of alternative views and will have to contend with challenges to their own positions.

In many ways, students learn how to write about literature by talking about literature. During the course of a semester, students will have relatively few experiences in writing an essay about a work of literature, but every day, students can engage in conversations that ask them to practice the same intellectual moves that are part of writing an essay. A specific purpose (i.e., advance an argument about a text) guides the practice, and feedback from peers helps learners to refine their arguments.

If the writing about a work of literature attends to a genuine problem of interpretation or evaluation, the prompts for the writing should follow logically from the preparation for encountering the text and from a series of extensive discussions. Two sets of contrasting prompts appear below. Consider what makes them distinct from each other.

Romeo and Juliet prompt #1: In a fully developed essay, explain who is mostly responsible for the tragic end of Romeo and Juliet. Be sure that your essay has a clear and unified thesis statement. In each body paragraph, be sure to support each of your observations with two quotes from the text. Be sure to use precise MLA style in citing the passages from the play.

Romeo and Juliet prompt #2: As we have seen with our own class discussions, many readers have disagreed about how to read William Shakespeare's *Romeo and Juliet*. Is it a play that celebrates romantic love? Is it about the dangers of prejudice? Is it about the importance of honoring the traditions of family? Is it about rashness of youth? Is it a representation of how tragedy is likely to befall anyone? Is it actually a confused mix of comedy and tragedy, injecting tragic circumstances on an otherwise comic narrative? Show your readers that you are familiar with competing ways to read the play. In your own essay, identify what you think is a significant theme of the play. You may decide that there is more than one central theme. Your completed essay should discuss the following considerations:

- Frame the problem of interpretation by noting the limitations of some interpretations that you have heard and offer a brief statement about an alternative way to read the play and appreciate its effects.
- Briefly explain what at least one other reader has thought about the play. Drawing from class discussions, fairly and accurately represent how the reader could arrive at this judgment and evaluate its limitations as your way to transition into your own thoughts about the play.
- In a series of paragraphs, show how you arrived at your interpretation and appraisal of the play: (a) Show the pattern of behavior, images, situations, or comments that convey meaning or cause an effect on the reader. In each body paragraph make an observation about how the play is developed (e.g., "Shakespeare depicts the excruciating pain of losing a loved one as a victim of hatred.") (b) In each body paragraph, quote specific evidence from the play. Note who made the statement and include the Act, scene, and line numbers (I, 2,11–14) in parentheses. (c) In each paragraph, explain what each quote means by noting how it supports your claim.

To Kill a Mockingbird prompt #1: In the novel, Scout tells the story of Jem's and her growing up in Alabama in the 1930s. Growing up involves having several significant life experiences and learning from them. Pick out three particularly influential episodes in Scout's life, tell what happened, and explain how the experience helped Scout to learn important life lessons.

To Kill a Mockingbird prompt #2: Since its publication in 1960, *To Kill a Mockingbird* has been a favorite of teachers, and it is one of the most often assigned readings in schools. Some enthusiasts point to Atticus as a model citizen. Some readers applaud the idea that Jem and Scout learn many important life lessons. Other readers appreciate that through her novel, Harper Lee appears to condemn racially motivated injustice. But does the novel deserve to be celebrated? As our class discussions have revealed, some contemporary readers find fault with Atticus and see the novel as a kind of implied argument for incremental change toward equality for all. In your essay, offer an evaluation of the novel, with special attention to the current controversies about it. Your essay should have the features that we as a class have identified as distinguishing coherent and carefully crafted essays.

PREDICTABLE VS. PROVOCATIVE

Using Google, if a student used the search phrase *"Romeo and Juliet* essay prompt," the effort would obtain more than 1,720,000 possibilities. A search on Google for a *"To Kill a Mockingbird* essay prompt" will yield at least 1,170,000 choices. If teachers are not already sensitive to this kind of result, they should become aware that most of the essay prompts that students see in school are already on the Internet, with accompanying essays, often free for downloading. One characteristic of the first essay prompt in each pair of prompts above is that it is predictable, thereby inviting plagiarism. While you may not be an obsessive guard against plagiarism, it is likely that you want students to write their own genuine analysis, not recitation of what they judge the teacher wants affirmed, nor the copied and pasted elements from someone else's essays.

The second choices in the pairs of prompts above share the fact that they each frame a problem and allow for many possibilities in responding. Furthermore, the prompts *refer to the related classroom discussions.* As Graff (1992) has suggested, when writers can refer to an area of doubt or dispute in interpreting or evaluating a text, the writers elevate the significance of the contribution in the essay. That is to say that the writers are making the case that the essay offers a contribution in an area that is uncertain. Students are aware of this uncertainty (or uncertainties) because this is what had been discussed in class as a critical focus. The prompts ask writers to reference the discussion in order to represent and evaluate an alternative possibility. No essay available on the Internet will be able to reference the points of view that were explored in class. These kinds of prompts do not guarantee that students cannot plagiarize, but they certainly do not invite plagiarism.

INFORMAL RESPONSES AND THE FUTILITY OF QUIZZES

All writing that students produce about a work of literature do not have to be a formal academic essay. Many teachers see value in asking students to write their reactions, observations, and assessments in a journal or in prompting students to write their impressions and questions in the form of "exit slips." Such efforts can help teachers to assess how learners are interacting with a text and can prepare students for discussions and for more extended and formal written responses.

Quizzing students on their reading is a common practice. In thinking about the possible value of quizzes, consider an actual conversation with a student teacher. In a post-observation conference, the student teacher was reflecting on the current lesson and sharing her plans for the next day. The conversation went something like this:

Teacher: I am thinking that I should give the students a short quiz tomorrow.
Supervisor: Why do you think that is necessary?
Teacher: My cooperating teacher and I think that a lot of the kids are not doing the reading.
Supervisor: What gives you that impression?
Teacher: Well, few students contribute during discussion, or they don't seem to recall the reading.
Supervisor: So, from discussions you already know that many of the students are not reading. How will the quiz tell you anything different?
Teacher: I don't know. It will just confirm what I suspect. And maybe the thought of the quiz will get kids to do the reading.
Supervisor: OK. And when the results of the quiz confirm that students aren't reading, what will you do then to inspire them to read?
Teacher: I don't know. Maybe the quiz will get them to read.

Some teachers use informal assessments to judge the extent and quality of students' reading of the literature. At the same time, there is a kind of futility in the typical quiz, as illustrated in the exchange above. The teacher already knows that the students aren't reading. The quiz, with its implied threat of a failing grade, does little to motivate students who just don't want to read the assigned text. The teacher already knows what the quiz will reveal—that many learners are not reading. The important challenge is knowing what to do with this information. If the students aren't reading, why aren't they reading? How can the teacher inspire learners to read? How can the teacher help learners to recall what they read and draw complex inferences about the text?

In the end, the daily oral discourse can reveal how students are experiencing a text. Informal writing can help students to capture their thoughts and synthesize the ongoing discussions. The more formal academic essays, if written in response to genuine critical problems, can reveal much about what students know about the procedures for reading literary texts and interrogating their implications.

YOUR VIEW

As demonstrated in this chapter, discussions and written analyses are two common means of response to literature. Sharing responses in discussions and writing to express interpretations and evaluations are important instructional elements because they help learners to become aware of alternative possibilities and the procedures that they and other readers practice in constructing the meaning from text. But you and your colleagues may think of other possibilities for responding to literature. With a few of your peers, discuss the following instructional challenges.

1. To what extent do quizzes motivate students to read complex texts and reveal to teachers how the learners are experiencing literature? What is the basis for your judgment?
2. If the conventional academic essay is limited in allowing students to express how they respond to a work of literature, what do you see as more promising alternatives? If you would allow for many alternatives, how would you standardize the grading for products that can be quite diverse in form and length?
3. This chapter distinguishes between *discussions* and *recitations*. What distinctions do you see? To what extent does each form of classroom discourse have some merit? If there is value in each experience, when is the place for each one?
4. If you discern that many of the students in your class are not reading the assigned text, what steps would you take to encourage students to read?

Chapter 9

Expanding Conceptions of Literary Texts

Literary texts are not always simply conventional print texts but also include readable digital and graphic works that require skills that can help expand a reader's repertoire of generating, consuming, and enjoying stories. While many still love the printed fiction, drama, and poetry commonly assigned in high schools, the art of storytelling can take a number of forms, including the popular *Snapchat*, which illustrates that narrators can convey their stories without words.

This chapter focuses specifically on one graphic narrative in order to illustrate the idea that each genre of storytelling has its own features and qualities that makes its own demands on the reader. It is not enough to assign students to read a graphic novel (or simply encourage students to read the ones that interest them); teachers still need to teach the procedures for noting features of the text and constructing meaning based on the conventions of the specific narrative form.

While students might be reading a variety of graphic narratives, a few have become commonplace in high schools: *Maus*, *Persepolis*, *American-Born Chinese*, *Skim*, and *Darkroom*. Given that much of the narrative in each case is conveyed in pictures, it is easy for teachers to assume that students can pick them up and read the text with little preparation or support. The focus here is on David Small's *Home after Dark* to illustrate how a teacher might work with students in modeling how to follow the narrative, draw inferences about its provocations and implications, and interrogate its themes.

GRAPHIC NOVELS AND A LITERARY READING OF *HOME AFTER DARK*

As Phelan (2018) points out, the novice reader can expand upon the "affordances of wholly verbal print fiction," by adapting some of the ideas employed in the verbal medium and so, using the skills of literature analysis, also closely examine "those of a graphic medium" (p. 27). As with any narrative, a reader can begin with an authorial reading in which the reader recognizes elements that the author probably expected an imagined audience to notice. In addition, in recognizing a narrative as a novel of initiation, the reader can anticipate the structure, direction, and emphases of the narrative.

For the purposes of illustration, most attention here focuses on how characters develop, through what they do and say, through the ways that others speak about them and react to them, and through the ways they are literally drawn on the page. This attention to character is most useful for the high school students learning the procedures for reading literary texts critically, since learners often assess the quality of a narrative based on their judgments about the characters who inhabit it and because much discussion of literature in high school classrooms focuses on characters—their appeal, their interplay with other characters, their motivations, and the ethics of their behavior.

For starters, consider a few literary descriptions useful in understanding the differences among character descriptions and motivations in the graphic novel, *Home after Dark*. Complicating the old chestnut about flat and round characters, James Phelan uses the following three basic aspects of narrative to discuss characters (Clark and Phelan, 2020, p. 11). These concepts are useful for discussing *Home after Dark*.

TYPES OF CHARACTERS: SYNTHETIC, THEMATIC, AND MIMETIC

Clark and Phelan classify literary characters as *synthetic*, *thematic*, and *mimetic*. These labels and the concepts behind them are far more useful than talking about "flat" and "round" characters or *protagonists* and *antagonists*. In complex works of literature, characters are complicated and sometime ambiguous, and they can serve multiple functions, frequently at the same time. Here is a summary:

Synthetic Characters: flat figures, one-dimensional manikins who are often representations of a person employed by the author as a plot device, a kind of "formalistic component (or aspect) of character directed to its role in the larger construct of the text" (Clark and Phelan, 2020, p. 2). One example from Small's fiction is the character of Aunt June, who only appears once, speaks a few sentences, and then disappears forever. Her only "task" in the novel is to reject both her brother and her nephew in an early scene, thus forcing them (in the plot) to look further for work and to cope with a world that seems even more uncaring than either imagined (pp. 35–41). She is the second woman who says "no" to her brother, Mike, and to Russell, her nephew, when they ask for help. That is all we know of her, and she serves no other function in the novel.

Thematic Characters: characters who are representations of ideas, classes, values, or traditions; Phelan (1989) calls them "themes with legs" (p. 9). In this sense, Phelan (2005) thinks about *thematic* as "that component of character . . . [in] a narrative text concerned with making statements, taking ideological positions, teaching readers truths" (p. 219). An example of a thematic character is Small's character Mah Jian, Mrs. Mah Wen's husband, who, according to Mah Wen, "speaks no English but understands everything you say" (p. 54), but who ultimately represents to Russell, at times unwittingly, how to achieve both serenity and authenticity (pp. 58; 373). Mah Jian becomes the embodiment of Russell's ideas of serenity and authenticity.

Mimetic Characters: "mimetic refers first to that component of character directed to its imitation of a possible person, . . . and, second to that component of fictional narrative concerned with imitating the world beyond fiction, what we typically call 'reality'" (Clark & Phelan, 2020, p. 2). Mimetic characters are identifiable with recognizable traits, or dispositions, but may also develop over the course of the novel some complex motivations, like the main character Russell, who has to learn to grow up with little guidance from disappearing parents.

While those three descriptors may be suitably identified by specific aspects in a given figure, Phelan thinks the really useful character analysis is done by also labeling how and why the character-figure is actually employed in the text (or film). In *Home after Dark*, Russell may be seen as predominantly a mimetic character, one who struggles with several of the basic issues of life, and who grows, learns, and develops by overcoming his and life's shortcomings. Our dominant focus is on him and his moral education in a genre typically called a *bildungsroman*, or a novel of a young person growing up.

It will become clear as you continue reading this chapter, that Phelan has teased out three specific ways of separating characters' qualities (he calls *dimensions* and Clark calls *aspects*); however, in almost all complex tales, they are mixed and matched in complicated ways as characters *function* in the progression of the novel. The most interesting characters in a work of literature display combinations of the three major attributes, and in some fictions, a one-dimensional character may even be said to dominate, like *Moby Dick's* Captain Ahab.

In addition to attending to individual characters' dimensions, Phelan is also very interested in what they actually do in the novel (1989). Although their *dimensions* may be seen more readily if a given character is identified in isolation from the work in which he or she appears, what they *do* with them are their *functions* in the text(s). (See Hamlet's intellect; Jane Eyre's determination as each possesses dimensions.) Whatever attributes (or traits) a character may exhibit or possess, his or her function (i.e., in the *progression* of the narrative) is the particular application of that attribute through its narrative's developing structure. In brief, Phelan says that "dimensions are converted into functions by *the progression* of the work."

The distinctions between dimensions and functions allows us to see the principle that the fundamental unit of character is neither trait nor idea, neither the role nor the word, but rather what Phelan will call "the attribute," something that participates in at least potential form in the mimetic, thematic, and synthetic spheres of meaning simultaneously. In brief, Hamlet as a *mimetic* character, *provisionally labeled*, reminds us of intense living young people we have met, if not known, before. He is *also* Shakespeare's *thematic* representation of a powerful intellect, someone who is so intelligent that he sees too many alternatives to decide quickly on any course of action (thematic). He acts (his function, among others), as Shakespeare's *synthetic figure* of revenge, an injured son who, however slowly, becomes the late king's instrument for purging his soul in purgatory (synthetic).

FROM SHAKESPEARE TO GRAPHIC FICTION: SMALL'S *HOME AFTER DARK*

Moving now from Shakespeare to graphic novels or comic books may seem like a huge leap in storytelling esthetics, but, in fact, each offers relatively novice story consumers a variety of rewards, each in its own way. The discussion below explores how to read a serious and poignant illustrated tale by David Small—the author/illustrator of the earlier prize-winning *Stitches*—a graphic novel titled *Home after Dark* (Liveright, 2018). Published a decade after his nomination for the National Book Award for *Stitches*, Small's *Home after Dark* was created using an interesting mix of sparse dialog and hundreds of sketches and drawings, and like any integrated work of narrative, it must be completed in toto to feel the emotional tugs the story elicits from the reader/viewer (cf. Sacks, 2019).

As noted before, this novel may be labeled a *bildungsroman*, the genre of a young person growing up ethically and emotionally. The young person here is Russell, and his growth and development over time is the "dominant focus" of the work. However, in any tale of this kind, we are always interested to know, among other issues, who is "blocking" or even "neglecting" the development of this young person and who is helping, or enhancing, or strongly supporting him or her? This person and his or her role may be a major character in the "Rule of Dominant Focus" as well as that of the growing adolescent.

This novel is narrated by Russell, a thirteen-year-old boy who, apparently after years of trying to ignore his dad and mom arguing, begins one Christmas season "hearing my parents' real voices for the first time" (p. 9). They are drinking and arguing in the bitter fashion of a couple in the process of permanently separating. Russell is not merely losing his family, but shortly will be abandoned by his mother and she never appears in his life again.

NOTICING CHARACTERS' FUNCTIONS AND DIMENSIONS

One helpful way of understanding the characters at the beginning of the story is to understand both their dimensions and their functions. As emphasized in chapter 4, a teacher can reveal a mature reader's thinking about character through modeling processes of noticing, reflecting, and questioning, but then gradually encouraging students to do the same. Russell's father, Mike, is a veteran of the Korean War, and post-divorce, having custody of Russell, moves from the Ohio rust belt to California, looking to find a job and a better life. Although he should also be helping his son to understand and then cope with all the changes happening in both their lives, Mike has his own problems.

Mike's personality is a mixed set of *mimetic* issues (he's an alcoholic, with emotional problems, and a limited understanding of his son), and he may be suffering from PTSD from the Korean War, with the drinking a form of self-medication. He is also a *synthetic* figure, whose ultimate disappearance, like his wife's, constitutes the very ground of why Russell will have to learn how to grow up almost alone. Finally, in his almost willful neglect of his own son, he is a major figure, *thematically*, representing an uncaring world, a world populated by those not necessarily malevolent but rather, by many who are simply not invested enough in Russell to make a difference. Nonetheless, he and Russell display some mimetic qualities via Small's sketches as the reader/viewer attempts to comprehend his motivations.

NARRATIVE CONTINUITY AND NARRATIVE GAPS VIA THE GUTTER

In a story told as much by pictures, graphic visuals, and cartoon-like figures, we first watch Russell trying to see himself in the reflections of Christmas-tree ornaments (pp. 4–5) while, over several pages of drawings (pp. 1–9), not dialogue, his parents squabble during Christmas. No words are spoken; we just see drawings of Russell's not very happy face, first as reflections in tree ornaments, then full-length drawn shots of him listening to parental screams. Abbot (2008) observes: "The space between frames in a cartoon comic sequence is called 'the Gutter,' a form of narrative gap built into the medium of the comic strip. It is the space in which the reader imagines events unfolding in time" (p. 234).

David Small often uses those types of gutter images to indicate time repetitions or transitions in Russell's life, and they will repeat, for example, shortly after his father disappears (pp. 262–63). What's interesting is how this particular graphic novel synthesizes both the brief language of Russell's voice—sometimes spoken out loud; some merely internal, self-narration—and how the graphic images, both of realistic scenes and images projecting Russell's fears, smoothly integrate both the real and the imagined. Russell's narrative voice and Small's sketches and drawings sometimes reinforce some element of the story; at other times, they act as counterpoint, and it is up to the reader/viewer to distinguish between and among them. In addition, the episodes in Russell's life are typically compacted into single chapters of the seventeen constituting the whole novel.

For example, look carefully at the drawings in Chapter One. The first scenes are shots of Russell's looking at the road and the garish advertising during the first few days of his and his father's trip to California. After seeing pictures of grubby and decaying Midwestern rust belt scenes, they stop for the night, displaying realistically distant sleeping arrangements in the first motel (p. 22). In the morning, Russell spots a starving and lonely puppy. Russell feels sympathy for the abandoned puppy but his father's immediate response is one word—no.

Noting all that follows, do we see a real or imagined shot of the puppy—alone in the middle of a highway, and a passing truck that may or may not have run over and killed it. How would we know at this point in the story if what we see is Russell's fantasy in the drawing following everything after

Mike's gruff "no"? What mimetic attributes should we ascribe to Russell: sensitive, lonely? What about the puppy? What thematic function does its short life represent in the story? How do we know? Again, what did the author probably expect readers to notice? By what rules can we confidently apply certain meanings to the graphic images, just as we would with conventional print text?

CHARACTER MOTIVES

Much is up to the reader/viewer in this scene, and indeed in many places in the whole of the graphic novel. In responding to characters in literary works generally, some critics like David S. Miall (1988) think our attention should be focused more on a character's motives instead of the traits (or trait lists) that might oversimplify matters in a "character chart." Here are some questions that the scene invites, as a teacher might demonstrate to a class.

1. So, describe what Russell's needs are here. For himself or for the puppy?
2. What might he need or want here from his father?
3. A little later, what does he seem to need from Aunt June?
4. How do you know these motivations? Verbal, or visual, or both?
5. Aunt June may be a plot device, a synthetic character never seen again. Since characterization can be built by familial associations, how could a reader speculate later (pp. 96–104) about understanding Mike via his Aunt June?

While Russell's father could be mostly a synthetic character, Mike displays some mimetic qualities as seen via Small's drawings or feelings via Russell's thirteen-year-old emotional filters. Do you have any reactions to Mike (pp. 42–43), or feel any emotional engagement with him, as well with Russell's needs (pp. 24–26)?

In many novels of initiation (*bildungsromen*), the hero of the story often considers his parents as mere adjuncts or contributors to his growth and development. However, in the more complex tales, the parents' values are part of the internal nature of the young character, and those qualities cannot be separated easily, as some youths believe for a time (cf. Shen, 2017, pp. 125–45).

The father, Mike, is an ex-GI who seems to demonstrate a mix of personality problems and some talents, and is portrayed mostly as not understanding ordinary human behavior and feelings very well, not those of his (now) ex-wife, his sister June, nor his own son, whom he often just ignores. He finally rents some rooms from a Chinese couple, Mr. Jian Mah and his wife, Mrs. Wen Mah. Russell, trying to familiarize his new world, watches Mr. Mah doing his exercises, the *T'ai Che*. He thinks, "California, would I ever get used to it?" (58) Mike has made a typical parental mistake—from a kid's point of view—of moving before school begins, supposedly avoiding loss of class time.

During this fallow time for Russell, his father has searched—and found—a new job: teaching basic English to prisoners at San Quentin Prison. He proudly announces it to his son and to the Mahs. Mrs. Mah offers to celebrate with a toast. Note the related drawing. Given the *rule of dominant focus* (character to whom an audience is to devote the majority of its attention), Mike seems far more important to Russell than either Mrs. or Mr. Mah or any other character so far. However, recalling the idea of the progression and the evolution of characters in complex stories, the reader must ask: What does Russell most need now in the story and whose mimetic qualities best represent what he needs?

A NEW LIFE FOR RUSSELL AND MIKE

Russell narrates in chapter 4 that, with the new job and the GI Bill (Federal loans for veterans after World War II and the Korean War), Mike buys a new house, albeit without much furniture. Note too that Russell is still alone until school begins. Mike seems oblivious that school-going is the easiest way for Russell to make new friends. As "the new kid," Russell encounters racist neighbors warning him not to associate with his Chinese landlady (pp. 69–70). Even more worrisome, they may have abused and killed animals—like the three kittens hung inside fences (pp. 75–76). These new events and images raise more questions:

1. Do you see any thematic or synthetic relationship between these dead kittens and Russell's scenes with the starving puppy?
2. How does his father respond to Russell's questions and fears?
3. Looking at the drawings, how do you as reader react to Mike's response: "Probably just some kids messing around"?
4. Why does Mike tell Russell (p. 78): "For god's sake stop being such a wimp"?
5. Note what could be called in a film the "jump cut" from p. 78 to p. 79. Assume you react more to either Russell or Mike, why does Small make such an abrupt change in your feelings in the gutter between the two pages?

Unfortunately, before classes begin, Russell still spends a lot of time on his own, watching TV kids shows and trying to please his father by keeping his dinner warm. Mike still seems unhappy. This situation invites other questions:

1. Why would he parody Russell's attempts to keep his dinner warm with the remark of the "last thing I need is my son becoming a hausfrau"?
2. Note the close-up picture (bottom of p. 95). In Russell's dream, what connections do you see between it and Mike's response to the club member who asks, "Say Mike, isn't that your son?" (p. 99).
3. What meanings do you derive from the visual images for Russell during the next several pages—detailing Russell's dream working as a waiter at the Lion's Club? Why do you suppose he ends up in the lion's mouth?

PLANTING AND PAYOFF WITH NEW FRIENDS

Chapter Five opens with Russell turning outward, but instead of safely exploring both his landlady's usually empty house and their surrounding environment, he investigates a new location, meeting Willie and Kurt, who show him "paradise," a muddy culvert under the road where they play a version of stickball. Making friends quickly, Russell asks them to meet him on their way to school, only to be reminded by Kurt that their social class differences make that impossible during school time.

One might argue here that Kurt's semi-rejection is a "plant"—"a preparatory narrative device that anticipates a future plot outcome"—by author David Small, and his character's "payoff"—"an outcome that typically resolves one or more storylines, or else draws on planted information to fulfill a narrative pattern"—could become very important near the end of the novel (Berliner, pp. 105–6).

As "the alien" in the public school, Russell is beaten up by aggressive middle schoolers, while many of the other kids just tend to ignore him. So, the next three chapters form a set of lessons for Russell, lessons difficult enough for kids who can turn to parents for advice. Most kids need help in dealing with the social environment at school during the ages of puberty, and near-adult ethical and social developments.

Following his being beaten up by the local pimple-faced bully, Russell encounters Warren, whose advice seems like a considered alternative to beating others or be beaten by them: Warren became invisible—and alert readers will note that, while such a strategy may be better than bruises and a regular split-lip, it too has limitations. Warren exhibits some unusual attributes: a good shot with a rifle and possessing as a pet a tamed rat carried inside his shirt pocket; nonetheless, he's friendly, seems to have lots of spending money to share, and—as Russell learns—they are both worried about being or becoming orphans.

As Russell discovers, Warren's being raised by his "grandma," a sympathetic but seeming distant authority who just hands him lots of money as compensation. Russell cannot help but contrast Warren's life with his own, being raised by his drunken and even more distant father. Although sharing some common fears, Russell quickly learns that Warren is, regrettably, more of an outcast than he—and reiterates his own dream by comparing Warren's social standing, not just with his own but with the in-crowd around them both. Readers should not be too surprised when Russell thinks to himself: "I must admit, it did make me wonder if I should risk being seen with a kid who wore trinkets and carried around a rat in his shirt" (p. 147).

Trinkets and rats aside, the most difficult experience Russell has with Warren is the latter begins making homoerotic suggestions that puzzle Russell, who, for the promise of two dollars, agrees to one minor experience. It scares him (pp. 160–72), however, and he distances himself from Warren (pp. 172–75), losing his only real friend. He moves away from sitting near him in school, and fortunately, meets up with Willie and Kurt just as summer vacation begins.

CONTINUED GROWING, LEARNING WITH FRIENDS TRUE AND FALSE

Russell's adventures with Kurt and Willie in the opening of Chapter Nine (p. 182) seems to presage a very good summer for all three. However, Russell is still growing and learning—to smoke cigarettes, to take risks on his bicycle with Kurt, who is also defined in mixed terms—mimetically and thematically a risk-taker, more so than either Russell or Willie. Kurt's flirting with a much older waitress in the local hangout seems confusing to Russell, at age thirteen; and his seemingly arcane knowledge of sex and women's bodies, however wrong-headed, is new to Russell. At the end of the chapter, Russell dreams he has become Kurt, and actually merges into his body. Here are some questions a teacher might pose aloud for the benefit of students:

1. This is an interesting dream, represented by the drawings on pp. 200–207. What kind of dream is this supposed to be? More erotic, or a dream of fantasied identity switches? Why does he want to look like Kurt?
2. Whichever a reader might think, what does Russell think about his dream (pp. 204–7), and why?

Opening Chapter Ten, the group plays stickball in front of the tunnel opening under the road and begin criticizing one another using anti-gay slang and insults not uncommon at that age and at that time. Russell reacts with surprising anger to one of Kurt's remarks (217), throwing a fast ball right at him. Later that evening, "in a moment of drunken earnestness," he told Kurt and Willie about Warren and the "hugging thing," and such news does not go well with them. He reflects (pp. 220–22) in pictures about his "confession," saying to himself out loud: "So. This was the price you paid for letting the world in." And a little later: "A single misstep, a wrong word, and you're a reject, a freak" (p. 223). This reflection prompts other questions:

1. What does he mean and what themes keep occupying him?
2. What other drawings of specific places earlier in the novel remind you of the drawings on pp. 224–27, and why do you think so?
3. Explain what you think the author/artist expected you to notice about these drawings?

The half-way point in the novel is Chapter Eleven, pp. 230–57, and the trip to the beach with Mike and the three boys. Consider several questions about Russell's character, summarizing what the reader has learned about Russell's growth and development: Why did Small end the sequence with the news that Russell never saw his father again? Given what a reader knows about Russell's growth and development by this point in the novel, how do Wen's questions to Mike (p. 238) and his responses serve as a kind of "plant" for the end of the chapter? What motivates Kurt to tackle Willy, keeping him from helping Russell being caught in the riptide? What's Mike's concern when Russell is brought to him? Why did Small end the sequence abruptly with the news that Russell never saw his father again (p. 257)? These explorations prompt further questions:

1. What are some of the rather common problems Russell has faced that kids his age (13 to 15 years old) also face, and how did he cope, or not cope? Are there places in the growth *progression* where such problems stand out?
2. As with many graphic novels, the reader must pay as close attention to the specifics in artistic drawings and pictures as to the character's dialogues. Where, if anywhere, do you see places so far where some of the drawings serve as part of the *progression* stand out for you? [Cf. pp. 11, 106, 117, 135, 157, 227]

As the tale moves into Chapter Eleven, Russell narrates that "comments about my masculinity were put on hold when my Dad took me, Kurt, and

Willie to little China harbor for a weekend camping trip" (230). He leads the boys in bawdy songs that night in their tents, and next day, it turns out Mrs. Wen Mah's restaurant is nearby so they eat there. Mrs. Mah questions Mike about his looking for a new wife, "For Russell's sake? For your own sake?"

We see Russell's face but no response from Mike as he gives the boys some money to take out a boat while he continues to drink lots of beer. After a scary ride in the surf, one that Mike appears too drunk to even notice, Mrs. Mah persuades Mike to let Kurt drive them back home, while he keeps singing his bawdy songs. Once home, Mike staggers off to bed, only ultimately to disappear, as the boy's mother did. Russell says that that night "was the last time I ever saw my father" (257).

WHAT DOES A PARENTLESS CHILD DO?

Alone completely now, Russell lets the house turn into a garbage dump, mail pilling up, utilities finally turned off, and the only constant was Mrs. Mah's delivery: "food still appeared on the doorstep every evening like magic" (Chapter 12, p. 261). Russell sees his face in a mirror-like large spoon, that should remind the reader/viewer of earlier drawings (p. 5) and the context in which he looks at his own self. Russell reflects: "Most nights, I lay awake, listening for the sound of Dad's car in the driveway" (p. 266). The sound he finally hears is the car of a worried Mrs. Mah, who finds mail unread, no utilities, and the house "a pigsty" (pp. 270–71) that "smells awful in here."

She begs him to promise to come live with them, but he says later that "I hated to break my promise to Mrs Mah but I already had my plans . . . [and] never wanted to see this house, this street, this town ever again" (p. 273). Bravely, he'd go to Alaska where he could "start all over. Everything there," he is convinced, "would be fresh open, clean, and free" (p. 274).

One might think this plan would begin a brand new start for Russell but he still has some learning to do in his own town. His night sleeping in the tree house in Chapter Thirteen is interrupted by discovering Kurt making love to the waitress from the diner (pp. 188–89), but having done so unsatisfactorily, for her. Given Kurt's comments on Russell's masculinity, and Mike's criticism about Russell becoming a *hausfrau* (p. 95), maybe these themes reflect their own limitations rather than Russell's.

Returning to the tree house after being "certain Kurt was not coming back," Russell "felt an ache of loneliness and helpless confusion that kept [him] awake until sunup" (p. 283). What is a bit shocking for Russell the next day are two unfortunate discoveries. Kurt realizes that Russell knows about his abbreviated evening with the waitress, and Russell learns that Kurt knows (pp. 286–87), although Willie seems oblivious to the meanings each understands.

Russell's new life gets put on hold for a stickball game that leads to the major ethical crisis of the novel, connecting Kurt's defensiveness, Russell's sympathy for animals, and his major cri de coeur. Most important is Russell's witnessing Warren's "punishment" for just being who he is: a gay boy not quite ready to come out. Teachers should remind students that each of the four boys is hardly one-dimensional, but each shares Phelan's three descriptors of dimensions (mimetic, thematic, and synthetic) as the scenes with the dead dogs require us to explain—to ourselves if no one else.

Russell's text narrative, and mostly the drawings, reveals how the various personalities function in multiple ways in these scenes, and how that variety is so important to understanding the whole novel. Here are some questions for the reflective reader:

1. Consider the sequence of drawings on p. 287, and ask what they tell you about both boys.
2. Why would Kurt immediately feel such anger and conviction that Warren shot the dogs? Why does he seem to hate Warren so much?
3. How does Willie's tone toward Kurt surprise you (bottom right panel)? Why would you be surprised?
4. On p. 298, what does Russell's internal dialogue represent?
5. What are his choices? And what does Mr. Mah's gift of money make him think?
6. Discuss the so-called Kurt-Warren "fight" (pp. 314–33). What is important about the panels on p. 321?

As dramatically as Chapter Fourteen ends, Chapter Fifteen *alternatively* offers mostly static pictures of Russell's search for Warren, his discovery of what Warren has done, and Russell's emotional dash back to the Mahs.

1. Why would he respond by stealing money from Mr. Mah's stash semi-hidden in his closet?
2. Look closely at Russell's dialogue with the truck driver, and his final advice to his passenger who wants "to live without hurting anyone" (p. 358). Why is that "ok for a mollusk?"
3. Mrs. Mah offers Russell a place to stay and explains why he can't go back to his former house. She also tells him about Mr. Mah's anger at him because "[he] felt betrayed. He has treated you like a son" (373). What does Russell's response to Mr. Mah's source of anger mean? (p. 374)

THE *DENOUEMENT*

The story is now coming to the end, in what is often called the *dénouement* or the unravelling of the tale. Russell works at the Mah's seaside restaurant, returning the money he stole. He discovers who killed the puppies, what happened to Kurt, and tells us about losing not only Willie's friendship but adds up all the people he has "lost": "Dad and Mom, Kurt and Willie, and, of course, Warren." He is convinced that Mr. Mah's look was always accusatory, and while Mrs. Mah was always gentle, "her little wrinkle of concern" always revealed her "thought [that] I was a hopeless case" (381).

Russell thinks, again, of running away to Alaska but Mrs. Mah tells him that he and her husband are very much alike. What does she mean by saying that, for Mr. Mah, "his only home is in the food he cooks" (385)? Russell's knapsack on his back, he begins his Alaska journey but starts by his retreating to the garden in Chapter Seventeen where "the garden at night [reveals its] tangled shapes simplified" (390), and again (cf. 58) watches Mr. Mah's *T'ai Che* (392–93).

Like so many novels of a young person growing up, narrative tension builds in the reader wondering what will help Russell cope with a very rough set of unfortunate life events. In the *denouement*, what are you seeing? The sketch of jungle-like drawing toward where Russell seems to be heading, but ends with the picture of the garden, where "it's tangled shapes are simplified" (389–90). Can you tell if Russell has emotionally grown and matured, or is he stuck again, feeling terribly sorry? What are the Mahs to him, and why "in the dark" does Russell say that he sees Mr. Mah's "strong sure steps moving away from harm" (p. 392)?

The teacher who works with a class to develop the disciplinary procedures for reading a graphic novel will want to explore how Russell's changes are internal and conveyed pictorially as well as verbally since coherence in graphic fiction is created by the synergistic mix of verbal and pictorial information. Hence, readers are invited to explain in detail what is in Russell's head. How do both Russell, the dominant character, and David Small, his creator, signal to us what and how these new and clarified thoughts have happened to the boy? If Russell's thinking has evolved, what does Mrs. Mah's last words in the novel (396), "Supper is ready," mean both to Russell and to you, the reader?

YOUR VIEW

When teachers study a graphic novel with learners, they have an obligation to work with the conventions that are unique to that form of literature and teach students how a mature reader constructs meaning. Perhaps you are already discussing with colleagues the unique characteristics of graphic novels.

1. How enthusiastic are your students about reading graphic novels? Which authors/illustrators are especially popular among the students you know?
2. What are some graphic novels that you have taught or that you hope to teach? What makes these forms of literary expression distinct from more conventional novels? What literary and visual skills have been necessary as you complete this whole work? How do you explicitly teach students how to work with the unique elements of a *graphic* text?
3. If you know students who are enthusiastic readers of graphic novels, why do these students find the form fascinating? How can you draw on their enthusiasm to influence their classmates to expand their reading and expand their conceptions of literature?

Appendix
Gary Soto's "Like Mexicans"

My grandmother gave me bad advice and good advice when I was in my early teens. For the bad advice, she said that I should become a barber because they made good money and listened to the radio all day. "Honey, they don't work como burros," she would say every time I visited her. She made the sound of donkeys braying. "Like that, honey!" For the good advice, she said that I should marry a Mexican girl. "No Okies, hijo"—she would say—"Look my son. He marry one, and they fight every day about I don't know what and I don't know what." For her, everyone who wasn't Mexican, black, or Asian was an Okie. The French were Okies; the Italians in suits were Okies. When I asked about Jews, whom I had read about, she asked for a picture. I rode home on my bicycle and returned with a calendar depicting the important races of the world. "Pues si, son Okies tambien!" she said, nodding her head. She waved the calendar away, and we went to the living room where she lectured me on the virtues of the Mexican girl: first, she could cook, and second, she acted like a woman, not a man, in her husband's home. She said she would tell me about a third when I got a little older.

I asked my mother about it—becoming a barber and marrying Mexican. She was in the kitchen. Steam curled from a pot of boiling beans; the radio was on, looking as squat as a loaf of bread. "Well, if you want to be a barber—they say they make good money." She slapped a round steak with a knife, her glasses slipping down with each strike. She stopped and looked up. "If you find a good Mexican girl, marry her of course." She returned to slapping the meat, and I went to the backyard, where my brother and David King were sitting on the lawn.

I ignored them and climbed the back fence to see my best friend Scott, a second-generation Okie. I called him, and his mother pointed to the side of the house where his bedroom was a small aluminum trailer, the kind you gawk at when they're flipped over on the freeway, wheels spinning in the air. I went around to find Scott pitching horseshoes.

I picked up a set of rusty ones and joined him. While we played, we talked about school and friends and record albums. The horseshoes scuffed up dirt, sometimes ringing the iron that threw out a meager shadow like a sundial. After three argued-over games, we pulled two oranges apiece from his tree and started down the alley, still talking about school, friends, and record albums. We pulled more oranges from the alley and talked about who we would marry. "No offense, Scott," I said with an orange slide in my mouth, "but I would never marry an Okie." We walked in step, almost touching, with a sled of shadows dragging behind us. "No offense, Gary," Scott said, "but I would never marry a Mexican." I looked at him: a fang of orange slice showed from his munching mouth. I didn't think anything of it. He had his girl and I had mine. But our seventh-grade vision was the same: to marry, get jobs, buy cars, and maybe a house if we had money left over.

We talked about our future lives until, to our surprise, we were on the downtown mall, two miles from home. We bought a bag of popcorn at Penney's and sat on a bench near the fountain watching Mexican and Okie girls pass. "That one's mine," I pointed with my chin when a girl with eyebrows arched into black rainbows ambled by. "She's cute," Scott said about a girl with yellow hair and a mouthful of gum. We dreamed aloud, our chins busy pointing out girls. We agreed that we couldn't wait to become men and lift them onto our laps.

But the woman I married was not Mexican but Japanese. It was a surprise to me. For years, I went about wide-eyed in my search for the brown girl in a white dress at a dance. I searched the playground at the baseball diamond. When the girls raced for grounders, their hair bounced like something that couldn't be caught. When they sat together in the lunchroom, heads pressed together, I knew they were talking about us Mexican guys. I saw them and dreamed them. I threw my face into my pillow, making up sentences that were good as in the movies.

But when I was twenty, I fell in love with this other girl who worried my mother, who had my grandmother asking once again to see the calendar of the important races of the world. I told her I had thrown it away years before. I took a much-glanced-at snapshot out of my wallet. We looked at it together, in silence. Then grandma reclined in her chair, lit a cigarette, and said, "Es pretty." She blew and asked with all her worry pushed up to her forehead: "Chinese?"

I was in love and there was no looking back. She was the one. I told my mother, who was slapping hamburger into patties, "Well, sure if you want to marry her," she said. But the more I talked, the more concerned she became. Later I began to worry. Was it all a mistake? "Marry a Mexican girl," I heard my mother say in my mind. I heard it at breakfast. I heard it over math problems, between Western civilization and cultural geography. But then one afternoon while I was hitchhiking home from school, it struck me like a baseball in the back: my mother wanted me to marry someone of my own social class—a poor girl. I considered my fiancé, Carolyn, and she didn't look poor, though I knew she came from a family of farm workers and pull-yourself-up-by-your-bootstraps ranchers. I asked my brother, who was marrying Mexican poor that fall, if I should marry a poor girl. He screamed, "Yeah," above his terrible guitar playing in his bedroom. I considered my sister who had married Mexican. Cousins were dating Mexican. Uncles were remarrying poor women. I asked Scott, who was still my best friend, and he said, "She's too good for you, so you better not."

I worried about it until Carolyn took me home to meet her parents. We drove in her Plymouth until the houses gave way to farms and ranches and finally her house fifty feet from the highway. When we pulled into the drive, I panicked and begged Carolyn to make a U-turn and go back so we could talk about it over a soda. She pinched my cheek, calling me a "silly boy." I felt better, though, when I got out of the car and saw the house: the chipped paint, a cracked window, boards for a walk to the back door. There were rusting cars near the barn. A tractor with a net of spider webs under a mulberry. A field. A bale of barbed wire like children's scribbling leaning against an empty chicken coop. Carolyn took my hand and pulled me to my future mother-in-law, who was coming out to greet us.

We had lunch: sandwiches, potato chips, and iced tea. Carolyn and her mother talked mostly about neighbors and the congregation at the Japanese Methodist Church in West Fresno. Her father, who was in khaki work clothes, excused himself with a wave that was almost a salute and went outside. I heard a truck start, a dog bark, and then the truck rattle away.

Carolyn's mother offered another sandwich, but I declined with a shake of my head and a smile. I looked around when I could, when I was not saying over and over that I was a college student, hinting that I could take care of her daughter. I shifted my chair. I saw newspapers piled in corners, dusty cereal boxes and vinegar bottles in corners. The wallpaper was bubbled from rain that had come in from a bad roof. Dust. Dust lay on lamp shades and window sills. These people are just like Mexicans, I thought. Poor people.

Carolyn's mother asked me through Carolyn if I would like a sushi. A plate of black and white things was held in front of me. I took one, wide-eyed, and turned it over like a foreign coin. I was biting into one when I saw a kitten crawl up the window screen over the sink. I chewed, and the kitten opened its mouth of terror as she crawled higher, wanting in to paw the leftovers from our plates. I looked at Carolyn, who said that the cat was just showing off. I looked up in time to see it fall. It crawled up, then fell again.

We talked for an hour and had apple pie and coffee, slowly. Finally, we got up, with Carolyn taking my hand. Slightly embarrassed, I tried to pull away, but her grip held me. I let her have her way as she led me down the hallway with her mother right behind me. When I opened the door, I was startled by a kitten clinging to the screen door, its mouth screaming "cat food, dog biscuits, sushi." I opened the door, and the kitten, still holding on, whined in the language of hungry animals. When I got into Carolyn's car, I looked back, the cat was still clinging. I asked Carolyn if it was possibly hungry, but she said the cat was being silly. She started the car, waved to her mother, and bounced us over the rain-poked drive, patting my thigh for being her lover baby. Carolyn waved again. I looked back, waving, then gawking at a window screen where there were now three kittens clawing and screaming to get in. Like Mexicans, I thought. I remembered the Molinas and how the cats clung to their screens—cats they shot down with squirt guns. On the highway, I felt happy, pleased by it all. I patted Carolyn's thigh. Her people were like Mexicans, only different.

References

Applebee, A. N. (1993). *Literature in the secondary school: Studies of curriculum and instruction in the United States.* NCTE Research Report No. 25. Urbana, IL: NCTE.

Applebee, A. N. (1996). *The curriculum as conversation.* Chicago: The University of Chicago Press.

Applebee, A. N., Langer, J. A., Nystrand, M., & Gamoran, A. (2003). Discussion-based approaches to developing understanding: Classroom instruction and student performance in middle and high school English. *American Educational Research Journal, 40*(3), 685–730.

Appleman, D. (2015). *Critical encounters in secondary English.* New York, NY: Teachers College Press.

Beers, K. (2003). *When kids can't read; what teachers can do: A guide for teachers 6–12.* Portsmouth, NH: Heinemann.

Berliner, T. (2019). Expect the unexpected: The types of planting and payoff. *Style, 53*(1), 105–29.

Booth, W. (1974). *A rhetoric of irony.* Chicago, IL: University of Chicago Press.

Bouque, A., & Forde, D. (2019). Troubleshooting discussion. In *Raise your voices.* Lanham, MD: Rowman & Littlefield.

Boyd, B. (2009). *On the origin of stories: Evolution, cognition, and fiction.* Cambridge, MA: Harvard University Press.

Canney, G., & Winograd, P. (1979). *Schemata for reading and reading comprehension performance.* Urbana, IL: Center for the Study of Reading.

Caracciolo, M. (2014). *The experientiality of narrative.* Berlin: De Gruyter.

Clark, M., & Phelan, J. (2020). *Debating rhetorical strategies: On the synthetic, mimetic, and thematic aspects of narrative.* Columbus: Ohio State University Press.

Dovey (2019, June 8). Can reading make you happier? *The New Yorker.* https://www.google.com/search?q=New+Yorker%2C+Can+reading+make+you+happier&rlz=1C1CAFA_enUS737US737&oq=New+Yorker%2C+Can+reading+make+you+happier&aqs=chrome..69i57j0.11816j0j7&sourceid=chrome&ie=UTF-8

Ericsson, A. (2017). *Peak: Secrets from the new science of expertise*. New York, NY: Houghton Mifflin.

Forde, D. (2019). Seeing and hearing what actually happens. In *Raise your voices*. Lanham, MD: Rowman & Littlefield.

Gee, J. P. (2007). *What video games have to teach us about learning and literacy*. New York, NY: Palgrave/Macmillan.

Gewertz, C. (2012). Common standards ignite debate over student "prereading" exercises. *Education Week, 31*(29), 1, 22–23.

Gillespie, T. (2010). *Doing literary criticism: The cultivation of thinkers in the classroom*. Portland, ME: Stenhouse.

Gladwell, M. (2011). *Outliers: The story of success*. New York, NY: Little, Brown and Company.

Goethe's Faust: Part one. (1808/2018). New York: Dover.

Graff, G. (1993). *Beyond the culture wars: How teaching the conflicts can revitalize American education*. New York, NY: W. W. Norton.

Graff, G. (2003). *Clueless in academe: How schooling obscures the life of the mind*. Hartford, CT: Yale University Press.

Graff, G. (2009). The unbearable pointlessness of literature writing assignments. *The Common Review, 8*(2), 6–12.

Graff, G., & Phelan, J. (2000). *The tempest: A case study in critical controversy*. Boston: Bedford St. Martin's Press.

Hartman, G. (1972, May). The mystery of mysteries. *New York Review of Books, 18*(9), 31–34.

Hattenhauer, D. (1998). The politics of Kurt Vonnegut's "Harrison Bergeron." *Studies in Short Fiction, 35*, 387–92.

Hillocks, G., Jr., McCabe, B., & McCampbell, J. (1971). *The dynamics of English instruction: Grades 7–12*. New York, NY: Random House.

Holmes, A., & Galchen, R. (2014, October 30). 'The Giving Tree': Tender story of unconditional love or disturbing tale of selfishness? *New York Times*. Accessed July 8, 2020. https://www.nytimes.com/2014/10/05/books/review/the-giving-tree-tender-story-of-unconditional-love-or-disturbing-tale-of-selfishness.html

Johannessen, L. R. (1992). *Illumination rounds: Teaching the literature of the Vietnam War*. Urbana, IL: NCTE.

Johannessen, L. R., Kahn, E. A., & Walter, C. C. (2009). *Writing about literature, revised and expanded edition*. Urbana, IL: NCTE.

Keen, S. (2003). *Narrative form*. New York: Palgrave.

Keen, S. (2007). *Empathy and the novel*. New York: Oxford University Press.

Langer, J. A. (2001). Beating the odds: Teaching middle and high school students to read and write well. *American Educational Research Journal, 38*(4), 837–80.

Lortie, D. (1977). *Schoolteacher: A sociological study*. Chicago, IL: University of Chicago Press.

Mandler, J., & Johnson, N. (1977). Remembrance of things parsed: Story structure and recall. *Cognitive Psychology, 9*, 111–51.

McCann, T. M. (2014). *Transforming talk into text: Argument writing, inquiry, and discussion, grades 6–12*. New York: Teachers College Press.

McCann, T. M., D'Angelo, R., Galas, N., & Greska, M. (2015). *Literacy and history in action: Immersive approaches to disciplinary thinking, grades, 5–12*. New York: Teachers College Press.

McCann, T. M., & Flanagan, J. M. (2002). A *Tempest* project: Shakespeare and critical conflicts. *English Journal, 91*(1), 31–39.

McCann, T. M., Flanagan, J. M., Johannessen, L. R., & Kahn, K. (2006). *Talking in class: New directions for classroom discussion*. Urbana, IL: NCTE.

McCann, T. M., Kahn, K., & Walter, C. C. (2018). *Discussion pathways to literacy learning*. Urbana, IL: NCTE.

McCann, T. M., & Knapp, J. V. (2019). *Teaching on solid ground: Knowledge foundations for the teacher of English*. New York, NY: Guilford Press.

Miall, D. S. (1988). Affect and narrative: A model of responses to stories. *Poetics, 17*, 250–72.

Nystrand, M. (1997). *Opening dialogue: Understanding the dynamics of language and learning in the English classroom*. New York, NY: Teachers College Press.

Phelan, J. (1989). *Reading people, reading plots: Character, progression, and the interpretation of narrative*. Chicago, IL: University of Chicago Press.

Phelan, J. (1996). *Narrative as rhetoric: Technique, audiences, ethics, ideology*. Columbus, OH: Ohio State University Press.

Phelan, J. (2018). Authors, resources, audiences: Toward a rhetorical poetics of narrative. *Style, 52*(1 & 2), 1–34.

Pichert, J. W., & Anderson, R. C. (1976). *Taking different perspectives on a story*. Technical Report No. 14. Urbana, IL: Center for the Study of Reading.

Pound, E. (1934/1958). *The ABC of reading*. New York: New Directions.

Rabinowitz, P. (1987). *Before reading: Narrative conventions and the politics of interpretation*. Columbus: Ohio State University Press.

Rabinowitz, P. (2014). Euclid at the core: Recentering literacy education. *Style, 48*(1), 1–111.

Rabinowitz, P., & Smith, M. W. (1998). *Authorizing readers: Resistance and respect in the teaching of literature*. New York, NY: Teachers College Press.

Rawls, J. (1971/1999). *A theory of justice*. Cambridge, MA: Harvard University Press.

Reed, P. (2000). Hurting 'til it laughs. In Leeds, M., & Reed, P. (Eds.), *Kurt Vonnegut: Images and representations* (pp. 19–38). Westport, CT: Greenwood.

Rogers, C. (1975). Empathetic: An unappreciated way of being. *The Counseling Psychologist, 2*, 2–10.

Rousseau, Jean-Jacques. (1763/1979). *Emile, or on education*. Intro., Translation, and Notes by Allan Bloom. New York, NY: Basic Books.

Sacks, A. (2019, June 26). Why we shouldn't teach literature with excerpts. *Education Week*. Accessed July 18, 2020. https://www.edweek.org/tm/articles/2019/06/26/why-we-shouldnt-teach-literature-with-excerpts.html

Sandel, M. J. (2009). *Justice: What's the right thing to do?* New York, NY: Farrar, Straus, and Goroux.

Schatt, S. (1976). *Kurt Vonnegut, Jr.* Boston, MA: Hall.

Seuss, Dr. (1958). *Yertle the turtle and other stories*. New York, NY: Random House.

Shanahan, Timothy. (2013a). Letting the text take center stage: How the Common Core State Standards will transform English language Arts instruction. *American Educator, 37*(3), 4–11, 43.

Shanahan, Timothy. (2013b). The common core ate my baby and other urban legends. *Educational Leadership, 70*(4), 10–16.

Shanahan, Timothy. (2019). My two-handed opinion teaching novels. *Reading Rockets*, from "Shanahan on Literacy." http://www.readingrockets.org/blogs/shanahan-literacy/my-two-handed-opinion-teaching-novels

Shen, D. (2017). Joint functioning of two parallel trajectories of signification: Ambrose Bierce's "A horseman in the sky." *Style, 51*(2), 125–45.

Shesgreen, S. (2009). Canonizing the canonizer: A short history of the *Norton Anthology of English Literature*. *Critical Inquiry, 35*(2), 293–318.

Showalter, Elaine. (2003). *Teaching literature*. Malden, MA: Wiley-Blackwell.

Smagorinsky, P. (2018). *Teaching English by design, second edition: How to create and carry out instructional units*. Portsmouth, NH: Heinemann.

Smagorinsky, P., & Fly, P. K. (1993). The social environment of the classroom: A Vygotskian perspective on small group process. *Communication Education, 42*, 159–71.

Smagorinsky, P., & Gevinson, S. (1989). *Fostering the reader's response: Rethinking the literature curriculum, grades 7–12*. Palo Alto, CA: Dale Seymour Publications.

Smagorinsky, P., Johannessen, L. R., Kahn, E. A., & McCann, T. M. (2012). *Teaching students to write fictional narratives*. Portsmouth, NH: Heinemann.

Smagorinsky, P., Kern, S., & McCann, T. (1987). *Explorations: Introductory activities for literature and composition, 7–12*. Urbana, IL: NCTE.

Small, D. (2018). *Home after dark: A novel*. New York: Liveright.

Smith, H. (2015). *Teaching particulars: Literary conversations in grades 6–12*. Philadelphia, PA: Paul Dry Books.

Smith, M. W. (1991). *Understanding unreliable narrators*. Urbana, IL: NCTE.

Smith, M. W., & Wilhelm, J. D. (2002). *Reading don't fix no Chevies: Literacy in the lives of young men*. Portsmouth, NH: Heinemann.

Soto, G. (1986). Like Mexicans. In Soto, G. (Ed.), *Small faces*. Houston, TX: Arte Público Press.

Vermeule, B. (2010). *Why do we care about literary characters?* Baltimore, MD: Johns Hopkins University Press.

Vonnegut, K. (1961, October). Harrison Bergeron. *Magazine of Fantasy and Science Fiction*, pp. 5–10.

Weissman, G. (2016). *The writer in the well: On misreading and rewriting literature*. Columbus, OH: Ohio State University Press.

Zajonc, R. B. (1968). Attitudinal effects of mere exposure. *Journal of Personality and Social Psychology, 9*(2, Pt.2), 1–27.

Index

Abbot, 130
accountability, of students, 11
active reading and meaning-making, 54–56
The Adventure Channel, 83
The Adventures of Huckleberry Finn (Twain), 21, 95
Ahmed, S., 77
All American Boys (Kiely and Reynolds), 31
Anderson, R. C., 97
"The Answer Is No" (Mahfouz), 92
Applebee, A., 1
assignments, significance of, 20–21
"The Attitudinal effects of mere exposure" (Zajonc), 20
attraction, rule of, 85
attribute, significance of, 128
Austen, J., 77
authorial reading, 47, 57, 72, 126

Beers, K., 62, 63, 65
bildungsroman genre, 127, 129, 131
Bloom, B., 47, 63
Booth, W., 39, 40, 43
bounded strategic empathy, 7
Bouque, A., 81, 115

Canney, G., 56
"A Cask of Amontillado" (Poe), 92, 116

CCSS. *See* Common Core State Standards (CCSS)
character-narrators. *See* first-person narrative
"The Chaser" (Collier), 57–58
class meetings, 11
cognitive-rhetorical model, 13
cognitive science perspective, 2
coherence, 3, 7, 23, 63, 77, 110, 121, 138; of curriculum, significance of, 22
Common Core State Standards (CCSS), 1, 26, 27
competing critical views, of text: "Gertrude McFuzz" and, 99–101; "Harrison Bergeron" and, 101–2 (views of, 102–4); significance of, 95–96; from simple to complex tasks, 96–97 (pre-reading prompts for, 97–99); and *Tempest* (politics of power and colonization in, 106–8; post card strategy, 104–6)
configuration, 76, 88; rules of, 77–80, 85, 89, 91–93
Connell, R., 8
consonant first-person narrative, 72
critical thinking, significance of, 113–14

Dark Night Channel, 83
"Dead Men's Path" (Achebe), 92

dénouement, 138
Dickens, C., 71
dimensions and functions: distinction between, 128; noticing, 129–30
"The Dinner Party" (Gardner), 92
discordant narrator, 76
discussion, engaging in, 9–10; significance of, 11
dissonant first-person narrative, 72
downfall, rule of, 85

electronic media, significance of, xi
empathy, 8, 14, 44, 86; for characters, significance of, x, 7; literature as experience of, 19; of readers, 7; response, fostering, 35–36; significance of, 20
Empathy and the Novel (Keen), 7
entertainment, literature as, 17–18
Ericsson, A., 57
exploration and learning, literature as, 19–21
"Ezzat's Roman Connection" (Goushegir), 86–99

fairness scenarios, 33–35; empathic response fostering for, 35–36
Faust (Goethe), 68–69
fear, as motivator, 9
fictional autobiographies. *See* first-person narrative
first-person narrative, 72–75
Flowers for Algernon (Keyes), 37–38
Fly, P. K., 114
focalizing, 65
Food TV, 83
Forde, D., 81, 115
free reading, significance of, 61–62
Freytag's pyramid, 8
frontloading of complex text reading, 26, 27, 116

Gee, J. P., 62
generative learning, 22, 58, 77
genre, meaning and significance of, 63, 64, 68

"Gertrude McFuzz" (Dr. Seuss), 99; perspectives on, 100–101; significance of, 99–100
The Giving Tree (Silverstein), 96
Gladwell, M., 57
Goushegir, E., 86
Graff, G., 3, 21, 95, 101, 118, 121
Great Expectations (Dickens), 35
Grosz, G., 40
guide questions, significance of, 11
gutter, 130

Hamlet (Shakespeare), 24
Harmony Channel, 83
"Harrison Bergeron" (Vonnegut), 101–2; views of, 102–4
Hartman, G., 63
The Hate U Give (Thomas), 31
Hillocks Jr., G., 22
Home After Dark (Small), 126; character motives in, 131–32; character types, 126–28; continued growing and learning with friends in, 134–36; dénouement in, 138; functions and dimensions in, 129–30; graphic novels and, 126; narrative continuity and narrative gaps and, 130–31; new life for Russell and Mike in, 132–33; parentless child in, 136–37; plant and payoff in, 133–34; from Shakespeare to graphic fiction in, 128–29
Hughes, L., 9

inductive method, of teaching. *See* inquiry, literature study as
informal responses and futility of quizzes, 121–22
inquiry, literature study as, 21–23
inquiry-based group activity, 80–81
instructional approach, 9, 12–13
instructional conversations, 22
intelligence quotient (IQ), 38–39
"The Interlopers" (Munro), 92
IQ. *See* intelligence quotient (IQ)
ironic tone, recognizing, 39–41; speaker significance for, 41–43

Johannessen, L. R., 30
journey and return, rule of, 85
justice scenarios, 31–32; criteria application for, 32–33

Keen, S., 7, 70–73, 76

Langer, J. A., 22
"Lather and Nothing Else" (Tellez), 92
"Like Mexicans" (Soto), 54, 57, 70, 71, 141–44
literary texts, 125. *See also Home After Dark* (Small)
Love, Hate and Other Filters (Ahmed), 77

Macbeth (Shakespeare), 21
Maupassant, G., 5
May, H., 91
McCabe, B., 22
McCampbell, J., 22
meaning-making and noticing: rules of notice for, 52–53; rules of signification for, 53 (application and practice with, 53–57; learning sequence, 58; practice extension, 57–58); significance of, 47–51; small group dialogue and, 51–52
Merchant of Venice (Shakespeare), 31, 35
Miall, D. S., 131
mimetic characters, 127–29, 131
modeling and practice, 58; from beginning, 65–69; significance of, 61–65; from simple to complex, 77–78; technical literary language and, 70–77
"The Most Dangerous Game" (Connell), 8, 92

National Council of Teachers of English (NCTE), 1, 5
Native Son (Wright), 21
NCTE. *See* National Council of Teachers of English (NCTE)
"The Necklace" (Maupassant), 5, 92
notice, ix, 3, 13, 14, 36, 41, 136; of character's functions and dimensions, 129–30; competing critical views and, 98, 104; modeling, sharing, and practicing and, 61, 65–70, 72–77; patterns, structures, and complex inferences and, 82, 84, 88, 89, 91; responding to literature and, 117, 126. *See also* meaning-making and noticing
Nystrand, M., 66, 110

"Of Arms and the Wall" (May), 89–91
The Outsiders (Hinton), 35

Paradise Lost (Milton), 69
paraphrasing, significance of, 34, 113, 114
"The Path Through the Cemetery" (Ross), 92
patterns and structures, and complex inferences, 79–81; "build your own movie treatment" (basic premise, 81–82; direction, 82–83; expectation, 83–86; practice with rules, 86); "Ezzat's Roman connection" and, 86–89; "Of Arms and the Wall" and, 89–91
peers, xi, 3, 16, 22–24, 45, 83; noticing and, 54, 57, 59; responding to literature and, 114, 119, 123
perpetual tension, rule of, 85
Phelan, J., 64–65, 72, 126–28
Pichert, J. W., 97
plant and payoff, 133–34
Pound, E., 61
practice, with rules, 86
pre-reading activities, 14; design principles for, 43–45; do's and don'ts of, 27–28; and fairness scenarios, 33–35 (empathic response fostering, 35–36); features of useful, 28–29; and justice scenarios, 31–32 (criteria application, 32–33); purpose-driven design for, 29–30, *30* (tapping into prior knowledge, 30–31);

"Reclamation and Renewal" case and, 36–37 (experience of narrative challenges and arguments and, 37–39; interpretation procedures and practices, 39–41); significance of, 26–27; speaker significance for irony and, 41–43
pre-specified answers, 10
Pride and Prejudice (Austen), 77
prior knowledge, 48; activation of, 14, 32, 58; tapping into, 2, 30–31, 44
procedural knowledge, 22
progression, 64–65
prompts, for writing, 119–21; plagiarism and, 121; as related to classroom discussions, 121
purposes, to study literature, *23*

quizzes, 1, 2, 9, 26; informal responses and futility of, 121–22

Rabinowitz, P., 47, 63, 65, 68, 70, 85, 91–93
Rawls, J., 31, 32
read aloud/think aloud protocol, 54–56, 65
reading, of text, 1–3; assigning of, 9; frontloading of complex, 26, 27; literature study as skills building of, 18; silent, sustained, 11. *See also individual entries*
reading from memory, 68
Real-Life Drama, 83
recitation, of text, 1–3, 10, 11, 121; discussion and, 110, 113, 118
"Reclamation and Renewal" case, 36–37; experience of narrative challenges and arguments and, 37–39; interpretation procedures and practices, 39–41
"representation of consciousness", 70–71
responses to literature, 109–10; class norms and, 111–12; dialogue as illustrated and, 116–18; informal responses and futility of quizzes and, 121–22; predictable vs. provocative prompts and, 121; rudiments of, 111–12; whole class discussion, 112–16; written, fostering, 118–21
rhetorical perspective, 2
A Rhetoric of Irony (Booth), 43
Rogers, C., 19
Romeo and Juliet (Shakespeare), 21, 24; prompts for, 119–20

Sandel, M., 31
Satire Central, 83
Scholes, R., 6
self-narration. *See* first-person narrative
self-reflection, 45
sequence for literature study, in high school, 14–16, *15*
Shanahan, T., 11, 26, 27
signification/significance, 15, 76, 77, 95, 121; literature experience and, 25, 36, 37; patterns, structures, and complex inferences and, 83, 89, 91, 92; rules of, 53 (application and practice with, 53–57; learning sequence and, 58; practice extension and, 57–58)
silent reading, sustained, 11
Silverstein, S., 96, 98
Smagorinsky, P., 30, 114
Small, D., 128, 130
small group dialogue, for meaning-making, 51–52
Smith, M. W., 21, 30, 43, 47, 85
"The Sniper" (Flaherty), 92
Soto, G., 54, 71–72
stances, in teaching literature, *12*
Stitches (Small), 128
Style (journal), x
success, rule of, 85
suspicion, rule of, 85
synthetic characters, 126–29, 131

A Tale of Two Cities (Dickens), 25, 35, 37
target outcome, identification of, 44

task analysis, completion of, 44
Teaching on Solid Ground (McCann and Knapp), ix
technical literary language, 70–77
Tempest (Shakespeare), 35, 104; critical conflicts as experience with, 104–6; politics of power and colonization in, 106–8
"Thank You, M'am" (Hughes), 9
thematic characters, 127–29
Things Fall Apart (Achebe), 35
Today's Detective, 83
To Kill a Mockingbird (Lee), 31; prompts for, 120
Twain, M., 95
The Twilight Zone (TV program), 65

"Unbearable Pointlessness of Literature Writing Assignments," 118

Understanding Unreliable Narrators (Smith), 43
unity. *See* coherence

vocabulary building, significance of, xi
Vonnegut, K., 101–2

Weismann, G., 14–15
Wilhelm, J. D., 21, 30
Winograd, P., 56
written responses to text, through reading, 14, 36

Yertle the Turtle and Other Stories (Dr. Seuss), 99

Zahn-Wexler, C., 20
Zajonc, R., 20

About the Authors

Thomas M. McCann is a professor of English at Northern Illinois University, where he contributes to the teacher licensure program. He taught English in high schools for twenty-five years, including seven years working in an alternative high school. His books include *Transforming Talk into Text* and *Literacy and History in Action*. His coauthored books include *Raise Your Voices: Inquiry, Discussion, and Literacy Learning* (2019), *Discussion Pathways to Literacy Learning* (2018), *The Dynamics of Writing Instruction* (2010), and *Teaching Matters Most* (2012).

John V. Knapp is emeritus professor of English at Northern Illinois University, and, continuing since 2007, the editor of the literary journal *Style*. Knapp has been an English teacher and a professor since 1963, educating students at every level from middle school to doctoral seminars. Knapp is the author and/or editor of several other books, including *Striking at the Joints: Contemporary Psychology and Literary Criticism* (1995), *Learning from Scant Beginnings: English Professor Expertise* (2008), *Critical Insights: Family* (2013), and over fifty articles and reviews on literature, family systems psychology, literary criticism, and literature instruction.

www.ingramcontent.com/pod-product-compliance
Lightning Source LLC
Chambersburg PA
CBHW022014300426
44117CB00005B/189